D1330034

Green Tea

Appreciating Chinese Tea

Written by Li Hong

Translated by Zhu Jianhua Bai Chongshun

CHINA INTERCONTINENTAL PRESS

WORLD CULTURE BOOKS

图书在版编目（CIP）数据

绿茶：英文/李洪著；朱建桦，白崇顺译.
-北京：五洲传播出版社，2009.12
ISBN 978-7-5085-1742-1

Ⅰ.①绿… Ⅱ.①李… ②朱… ③白… Ⅲ.①绿茶-文化-中国-英文 Ⅳ.①TS971

中国版本图书馆CIP数据核字（2009）第216749号

Original Chinese language edition copyright © 2009 by China Light Industry Press

著　　者：李　洪
译　　者：朱建桦 白崇顺
选题编辑：荆孝敏 世界文化图书
责任编辑：王　莉 Lisa Zhang
装帧设计：宋索迪
设计制作：世界文化图书

出版发行：五洲传播出版社
地　　址：北京市海淀区北小马厂6号华天大厦
邮　　编：100038
网　　址：www.cicc.org.cn
电　　话：010-58891281
印　　刷：恒美印务（广州）有限公司
开　　本：889×1194mm　1/32
印　　张：5
版　　次：2010年1月第1版 2010年1月第1次印刷
07980（平）

Contents

Thanks to Jing Xiaomin, Li Mei, Madhumita Bardhan Sinha, Wang Li, Lisa Zhang and Suodi Song for their tireless efforts to make the project possible.

Since the first cup brewed almost 5,000 years ago, green tea's popularity has increased to the point that it is presently the second most popular beverage in the world. As the name suggests, the tea is green in color.

At first glance, all brewed tea appear the same, but a connoisseur is able to identify the different varieties of green tea through the appearance and color of the dried tea—the flat Long Jing tea; the snail shell-like outwardly curling Bi Luo Chun tea and the bamboo-green Zhu Ye Qing, all tell their own stories. The varied flavors of green tea, such as Bi Luo Chun tea's aroma of flowers and fruits; An Ji White Tea's fresh and mellow taste and the Yunnan big-leaf tea's impressive aftertaste that becomes sweeter with subsequent brewing add to the unique charm of green tea.

After being harvested, the fresh tea buds and leaves are processed into the tea that we see, taking care to retain the authentic flavor of the leaves. Despite the apparent differences between all its varieties, its simple and elegant nature is common to all green tea.

Each sip of the tea is a discovery in itself. Appreciate the "dance of leaves" while sipping a cup of green tea. You will find tranquility and peace even amid the humdrum of life.

Li Mei

Introduction to Green Tea

Part 1

Chinese tea may be classified in many ways. Categorizing according to processing techniques, we have the basic tea group and the reprocessed tea group. Basic tea group includes green, yellow, white, blue (Oolong), black and dark tea. Green tea is the closest to nature among all tea types.

1. Production Areas of Green Tea

Green tea is the earliest tea processed and consumed in China. It accounts for approximately 70% of China's total tea yield. In the international green tea market, China's contribution is 70% or greater. At present, tea plantations are found in 20 provinces, autonomous regions and municipalities including Yunnan, Guizhou, Sichuan, Chongqing, Hainan and Taiwan. The production areas are spread across more than 1,000 counties including Anhui, Jiangxi, Hunan, Hubei, Guizhou, Sichuan and Chongqing as the major areas, with relatively low yield from Guangdong, Guangxi, Fujian, Taiwan, Hainan, etc. Henan, Shandong and Shaanxi, north of the Yangtze River, too produce small quantities. In addition, some green tea plantations in northwest Gangsu and Tibet give small yields.

According to their distribution nationwide, China's tea plantations can be divided into four green tea production areas: south of the Yangtze River, north of the river, southwest China and south China.

Green Tea Plantation

Major Green Tea Production Areas and Famous Local Tea Varieties			
Production Area	**Famous Tea Varieties**	**Production Area**	**Famous Tea Varieties**
Zhejiang	Long Jing Tea, An Ji White Tea, Zhejiang White Tea, Organic Green Tea, Organic Cui Jian Green Tea, Kai Hua Long Ding, Xiangcha Tea	Hunan	Gao Qiao Yin Feng, Shi Men Yin Feng, Xiang Bo Lv
Jiangsu	Bi Luo Chun Shan	Shandong	Lao Shan Green Tea
Anhui	Huang Shang Mao Feng, Tai Ping Hou Kui, Liu An Gua Pian, Song Luo Tea	Guizhou	Mei Tang Que She, Mei Tang Cui Ya Tea, Du Yuan Mao Jian, Zun Yi Mao Jian
Sichuan	E Mei Zhu Ye Qing, Meng Ding Gang Lu,	Shaanxi	Wu Zi Xin Hao, Wu Zi Green Tea, Zi Yang Mao Jian, Zi Yang Cui Feng, Fu Xi Tea
Henan	Xin Yang Mao Jian	Guangxi	Ling Yuan Bei Hao, Ling Luo Chun
Jiangxi	Wu Yuan Ming Mei	Yunnan	Dian Qing

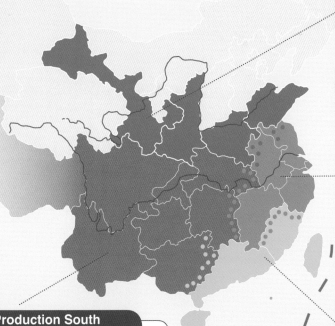

Green Tea Production South of the Yangtze River

With the longest history of tea plantation, this area boasts the most varieties of famous green tea in China. Vast plantation land and abundant natural resources make the green tea production area south of the Yangtze River, specifically Hunan, Hubei, Jiangxi, southern Jiangsu, southern Anhui, northern Fujian, Shanghai, etc., a major contributor. Many famous green teas are produced here, including Long Jing, Bi Luo Chun, Huang Shan Mao Feng, Wu Yuan Ming Mei, Gao Qiao Yin Feng, etc.

Green Tea Production North of the Yangtze River

The northernmost tea plantation area, it covers the terrace along the north of the Yangtze River and the south of the Mt. Qinling-River Huaihe, including Shaanxi, Henan, Shandong, etc., cultivating shrub-type tea varieties with small or medium leaves. The famous green tea varieties in this area include Wu Zi Xin Hao, Zi Yang Mao Jian, Bi Kou Long Jing, Ri Zhao Xue Qing, etc.

Tips

Bi Kou Long Jing tea is a famous green tea of Gansu Province.

Green Tea Production in the Southwest

The southwest is believed to be the original tea plantation area. With abundant tea tree resources of diverse varieties, the tea production area is in Yunnan, Guizhou, Chongqing, Sichuan and Xiangxi of Hunan, east Tibet, etc. The famous green tea varieties here include Nan Nuo Cha Bai Hao, Du Yuan Mao Jian, Zhu Feng Sheng Tea tea, etc.

Tips

Zhu Feng Sheng Cha tea is a famous tea in Linzhi Prefecture of Tibet.

Green Tea Production in South China

This area includes regions south of the Nanling Mountains such as South Fujian, Guangdong, Guangxi, Hainan and Taiwan, etc., that produces Oolong tea and green tea. The famous green teas of this area include Ling Yuan Bai Hao of Guangxi, San Xia Bi Luo Chun of Taiwan, etc.

2. Classification of Green Tea

Green tea is basic tea; however, it can be also sub-classified into the basic green tea group and the reprocessed green tea group. The basic green tea group comprises all crude tea and refined tea produced by green tea processing techniques, such as Long Jing, Bi Luo Chun and Huang Shan Mao Feng. The deep-processed green tea belongs to the reprocessed group mainly comprising scented tea, compressed green tea, green tea extract, fruit-flavored green tea, bag green tea, beverage and food with green tea ingredients, and polyphenol preparation with active substances extracted from green tea.

Classification of Green Tea	
By production areas	Zhejiang Green Tea, Anhui Green Tea, Sichuan Green Tea, Jiangxi Green Tea, etc.
By harvest seasons	Spring Tea, Summer Tea and Autumn Tea, of which Spring Tea has the best quality, Autumn tea is second, and Summer tea leaves are generally not picked. Dividing according to seasons, Spring Tea can be further classified into: before the Pure Brightness (April 5–6) at 15°and before the Grain Rain (April 20–21)at 30°.
By grades	Superior (first, second, and third superior grades), first, second, third, fourth and fifth grades.
By appearance	Green tea varieties are needle-like, such as An Hua Song Zheng, etc.; flat, such as Long Jing tea; some are spiral-shaped, such as Bi Luo Chun tea; slice-shaped, such as Liu An Gua Pian; orchid-flower-like, as Shu Cheng Lang Hua tea; single-bud shaped, such as Meng Ding Huang Ya tea; straight-lined, such as Nanjing Yu Hua tea; curve-lined, such as Wu Yuan Ming Mei tea, Jing Shan tea ; pearl-like, such as Ping Shui Zhu tea.
Text missing	Old famous tea and modern famous tea are represented by Gu Zhu Zi Sun tea and Nanjing Yu Hua tea respectively.
By processing techniques	The handmade (high quality) varieties are processed manually, but there are also some machine-processed or half machine-processed and half-manual green tea.
By quality-based brands	Famous green tea and common green tea.
By ways of deactivation and desiccation	Steamed, roasted, baked and sun-dried green tea varieties.

3. Classification of Green Tea by Processes

According to the science of tea, green tea is classified by the process of deactivation and desiccation.

1. Steamed Green Tea

The steaming technique for making cake tea was fully developed in the Tang Dynasty (618–907). Chapter Three of the *Classic of Tea* written by Lu Yu (760– 780) records the details. Lu Yu describes: "Pick the fresh leaves on a sunny day, and then steam, roll, pat, bake, pack and envelope. Cured tea cake is ready." As the oldest green tea variety, steamed green tea is still produced today, for example, the Yu Lu Tea from Enshi of Hubei Province.

Steamed green tea

Steamed green tea is processed through steam deactivation. The tea quality features "three greens," namely, green dried tea, green liquid and green brewed leaves. Most Japanese green tea, such as Sencha, Gyokuro and Tencha are steamed. In recent years, several steamed green tea production assemblies have been established in Zhejiang and Jiangxi, etc. The output is mainly exported to Japan, with a small quantity sold domestically, such as bag steamed tea and green tea powder.

2. Roasted Green Tea

Tea Song Lyrics of West Mountain Temple, a poem by well-known Liu Yuxi of the Tang Dynasty (618–907), is the earliest recordings of roasted tea marking the start of the tea-roasting process. However, at that time, cake tea was more likely the imperial tribute, especially in the Song Dynasty (960–1276) when "Long-Feng Tea Cake" was favored. The tea in bulk was only popular in south China.

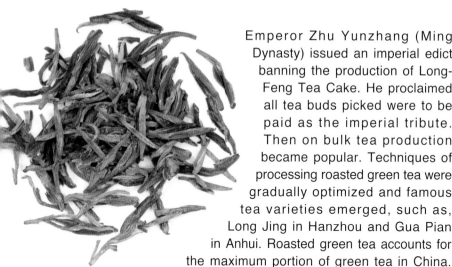

Emperor Zhu Yunzhang (Ming Dynasty) issued an imperial edict banning the production of Long-Feng Tea Cake. He proclaimed all tea buds picked were to be paid as the imperial tribute. Then on bulk tea production became popular. Techniques of processing roasted green tea were gradually optimized and famous tea varieties emerged, such as, Long Jing in Hanzhou and Gua Pian in Anhui. Roasted green tea accounts for the maximum portion of green tea in China. Desiccation of this tea can be either on manually operated pans or in roasters. According to the appearance of the dried tea, roasted tea can be classified into three sub varieties: long, round, and fine and tender.

Roasted green tea

Tips

Very high temperature may produce a "high flaming" or sometimes even a "burned" fragrance. The color turns more yellowish-green as compared with the tea roasted at normal temperature.

3. Baked Green Tea

In the initial processing, baked green tea is dried by baking over charcoal fire or in a baking machine.
Baked green tea base is generally used as the raw material for the scented tea.
The baked green dried tea features relatively whole buds and leaves and a prominent fuzzy petiole, clear and bright liquid, and a fruit or flower fragrance.

Tips

Traditional baked green tea is dried over charcoal fire. If not properly handled, the tea may absorb its smoky flavor.

Baked green tea

4. Sun-dried Green Tea

The sun-dried green tea is directly dried by sunlight—the oldest way of desiccation. Sun-dried green tea is mainly produced in Yunnan, Shaanxi and Sichuan. They are named after their respective places of production: Dian Qing in Yunnan, Shan Qing in Shaanxi and Chuan Qing in Sichuan. Mostly compressed as cake tea and Tuo tea (a bowl-shaped compressed mass of tea leaves), only a small amount is directly sold for consumption. Processing sun-dried green tea involves: deactivating the fresh leaves, rolling into striations and spreading over bamboo sheets in the sun. The most distinctive feature of this tea is its special sun-dried flavor.

Over the years, new processes have been introduced to better meet the market demand. For desiccation of some tea varieties, such as Wu Zi Xing Hao of Shaanxi and Kai Hua Long Ding of Zhejiang, roasting subsequent to baking or the contrary is applied to ensure a better fragrance and look. For some other tea varieties, such as E Meng Zhu Ye Qing of Sichuan, the tea buds and leaves are processed by steam deactivation and then are followed by the roasting and baking process. In some cases, the fresh green tea buds and leaves are deactivated in hot water and then are instantly scooped up for further processing.

Tips

The technique of instant dipping in hot water produces green tea with low content caffeine

Sun-dried green tea

4. Processing Green Tea

According to the *Classic of Tea*, the earliest, primitive habit of chewing fresh leaves gradually evolved to cooking the fresh leaves into a thick soup for drinking. People had already learned to bake the fresh tea leaves directly over a fire or in a bamboo canister prior to cooking in water. Even today, some ethnic minorities, such as the Dai and Wa living in Xishuangbanna Prefecture of Yunnan Province still retain the old ways of tea drinking—baking, cooking or brewing of the fresh leaves. They make a special tea known as Bamboo Canister Fragrance Tea by putting the baked leaves into freshly cut bamboo tubes, or the fresh tea leaves directly into a bamboo tube to bake, soften or burn before brewing for drinking. The tea liquid has a pleasantly smoked fragrance, bitter and mellow with a sweet aftertaste.

Today, the essential steps involved for processing green tea are picking fresh leaves → deactivation → rolling → desiccation, which produces the preliminarily processed green tea "crude tea."

Tips

Zhang Ji, a famous scholar in the Three Kingdoms period (220–280)records in his *Guang Ya* : "In the regions of Jing (present-day west Hubei Province) and Ba (present-day Chongqing municipality), tea cake is made with harvested tea leaves."

1. Harvesting Fresh Leaves

Fine tender fresh tea leaves, generally a single bud, a bud and a leaf or a bud and two leaves are picked for green tea processing. The tea leaf picking is such that it excludes impurities, such as old stems or leaves, flower buds and tea fruits. The leaves are not pressed hard or piled too high to ensure the fresh quality. Failure of proper management may turn the leaves unsuitable with reddened rims and stripes. The temporary storage yard is shady, cool, well ventilated and clean.

2. Deactivation

Deactivating enzymes in the fresh leaves prevents the polyphenolic enzymes from oxidizing and guarantees green tea's quality. The unpleasant smell evaporates during deactivation, leaving a floral fragrance. In traditional processing, deactivation is usually operated by roasting the fresh leaves in pans, while in modern times, especially for mass production, cauldron-type or cylinder-type deactivating machines are widely used. Rolling and baking follows deactivation. Deactivating involves the "alternative stir-frying of fresh leaves and stewing, with more stir-frying than stewing and longer duration of deactivating for more tender leaves than for the more mature leaves." The temperature of the cauldron-type deactivating machine is maintained at 180–250°C, and you can hear the blasting when the fresh leaves are thrown into the machine. The temperature control is "higher first and lower later." The per feed amount of fresh leaf is about 500–1,000g; the deactivating duration 5–8 minutes depending on the quality of the leaves. The cylinder-type deactivating machine takes in more fresh leaf feed; the deactivating duration is 2–3 minutes. For steam deactivation, the deactivating duration is much shorter—30–60 seconds, keeping the temperature above 95°C.

3. Rolling

There are two purposes of tea leaf rolling: to moderately crush the internal tissues of the leaves so as to let the internal substances penetrate up to the external surface and to mold the contour of tea so as to make the leaves and buds curl into required shapes. High-quality green tea is usually rolled by  hand. The more tender leaves are rolled after cooling the deactivated leaves while the less tender leaves are rolled when the leaves are still warm. The pressure on the tea is relieved in the later period of rolling, and finally, the clusters of the rolled tea are scattered to prepare for desiccation. For low and medium grades of green tea, rolling machines are generally applied.

4. Desiccation

Desiccation is baking, roasting and sun-drying the leaves to dry the moisture and develop the fragrance. In traditional processing, roasted green tea is dried in pans, baked green tea in baking baskets and sun-dried green tea directly by sunlight. Roasted green tea is usually more fragrant.

Column 1 Organic Tea

What Is Organic Tea?

Organic tea is a tea variety or related product certified by a competent organic tea certification agency. For organic tea plantation management, natural laws and biological principles are given priority. It promotes agricultural techniques conducive to eco-environmental sustainability, without use of any pesticides, fertilizers and growth regulators or other chemicals. It does not permit the use of any synthetic food additives.

Properties of Organic Tea

1. Agricultural production areas, are located in eco-friendly environments far from pollution.
2. The production of organic tea is free from synthesized pesticides, fertilizers, growth regulators, herbicides and other substances.
3. The whole process involves quality control—from production, processing, sales, etc.
4. In China, all organic tea products bear an exclusive stamp under the protection of *Trademark Law of the People's Republic of China* given only to products certified by the competent certification agency.

Organic tea is a safe, pollution free and top-quality drink whose production follows stringent regulations.

Organic Jasmine Tea

Currently, the output of organic jasmine tea is relatively small, partly due to serious insect attacks on the jasmines flowers and thus fail to meet the standard for organic agriculture. Organic jasmine tea certification needs to meet the following requirements: First, the tea base must be a certified one. Secondly, jasmine shall be planted and managed in accordance with organic agricultural standards that ban any use of synthesized substances during plantation. Last but not least, the maximum content of jasmine in the tea shall not exceed 5%, the pesticide residue amount shall be smaller than the minimum inspection limit and all indexes shall be tested and proved by the competent organic tea certification agency.

Organic Tea & Common Tea

The evaluation of common tea is generally determined by inspecting the finished tea products while seldom probing into plantation, processing and transportation, etc. For evaluation of organic tea, in addition to the inspection of the finished products, the most important consideration is to check whether the products are polluted during plantation, processing, packing, storage and transportation. Moreover, application of chemically synthesized fertilizers and pesticides are allowed for management of common tea plantations, while such substances are not allowed in the organic tea plantations. Furthermore, the quality problems in organic tea production can be investigated by tracing the records kept, which is not practical for common tea.

Mark of organic tea

A Survey of Famous Green Teas in China

Part 2

Long Jing, Bi Luo Chun, Huangshan Mao Feng, Xinyang Maojian—so many green tea types may confuse a novice tea drinker. This part will introduce all the famous brand names of green tea, giving information on their production areas, the characteristics of each type and how each type of tea is processed.

I. Famous Green Tea in Zhejiang Province

Located south of the Yangtze River tea production area, Zhejiang Province is an important base for green tea production. Tea plantations include Jiaxing, Hangzhou, Huzhou, Shaoxing, Yuyao, Jinhua, Cixi and Quzhou. The major famous green tea brands include Xi Hu Long Jing, Da Fo Long Jing, White An Ji, Chang Xing Zi Zhu, Jing Shan, Hui Ming, Xue Shui Yun Lu, Ling Hai Pan Hao, Yan Dang Mao Feng, etc.

1. Long Jing Tea "Dragon Well Tea"

Known as the "Queen" of green tea for its "green color, strong fragrance, mellow taste and pretty contour," Long Jing fresh green tea leaves are harvested before the Grain Rain of the Solar Term, and the typical sample of this tea is flat, tastes sweet with a fragrance of leguminous flowers. Traditional and modern high-quality Long Jing tea is completely manually roasted. Roasting of the Long Jing tea requires great attention and skilled hands during the tea-leaf processing. In 1757, visiting the South Yangtze area, Emperor Qianlong of the Qing Dynasty also commented upon the process of roasting in his poem *The Song upon Inspecting the Tea Craftsmanship*. Today, although roasting is usually performed with electric pans, the processing skills remain highly demanding. The harvested fresh leaves must be spread thinly on the ground to deactivate and roll (15 minutes); the deactivated and rolled leaves are spread for cooling and regaining moisture, ready to be sifted. Then they are desiccated and shaped in the pans. The desiccated crude tea is sifted and then re-roasted before the processed crude tea is sifted again to remove any residue fragments and dust. Finally, it is piled up and stored according to their grades.

Long Jing tea is a flat, smooth and bright green leaf, with a mellow and refreshing taste and a light aftertaste. The liquid is clear and bright, pleasantly fragrant and with evenly immersed and settled tea leaves at the pot bottom (henceforth referred to as brewed leaves). Long Jing tea is produced in three areas, namely, Xihu, Qiantang and Yuezhou, with such famous brands as Xi Hu Long Jing, Qian Tang Long Jing and Yue Zhou Long Jing.

Lake Xihu, Longwu, Liuxia, Zhuantang and Zhoupu of Xihu district of Hang Zhou City are home to Long Jing tea and the famous Xi Hu Long Jing. Both the picked and the processed varieties are collectively named after the place of origin, Lake Xihu (the West Lake).

Tips

Traditionally, Xi Hu Long Jing is packed in craft paper and stored in pottery jars along with some quicklime wrapped in a piece of clean cotton cloth.

The dried tea

The liquid

The brewed leaves

2. Shi Feng Long Jing

Shi Feng Long Jing is the best of Xi Hu Long Jing, which is the best among all Long Jing teas. It is also believed to be the most authentic Long Jing tea because of its place of origin from Long Jing town, surrounded by Mt. Shi Feng in the hilly Xihu District of Zhejiang Province.

The dried tea

The liquid

The brewed leaves

Long Jing white tea actually belongs to a green tea variety locally known as "Long Cha," mainly produced in the Anji and Pang'an counties of Zhejiang Province. Using the technique of Long Jing, the tea is processed from the fresh white tea leaves from local tea plantations.

The dried tea   The liquid   The brewed leaves

↑ High-quality Long Jing White Tea

The dried tea   The liquid   The brewed leaves

↑ Common Long Jing White Tea

4. Qian Tang Long Jing

Qian Tang Long Jing is the collective name for a Long Jing tea variety processed from fresh leaves picked from the counties and cities of Hangzhou, Xiaoshan, Yuhang, Lin'an, Chun'an, Fuyang, Jiande and Tonglu.

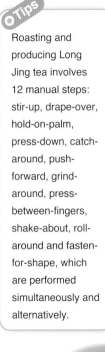

Tips

Roasting and producing Long Jing tea involves 12 manual steps: stir-up, drape-over, hold-on-palm, press-down, catch-around, push-forward, grind-around, press-between-fingers, shake-about, roll-around and fasten-for-shape, which are performed simultaneously and alternatively.

The dried tea

The liquid

The brewed leaves

5. Yue Zhou Long Jing

Yue Zhou Long Jing is the collective name for Long Jing tea variety processed from fresh leaves from the counties, districts and cities of Xinchang, Chengzhou, Shaoxing, Yuecheng, Zhuji, Pan'an, Shangyu, Dongyang and Tiantai. Tea production areas outside Zhejiang Province also produce Long Jing tea processed according to Long Jing tea techniques. The tea products appear similar to Long Jing tea, but after brewing, there are marked differences in fragrance and taste from the original Long Jing tea.

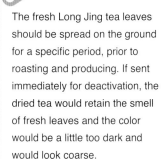

Tips

The fresh Long Jing tea leaves should be spread on the ground for a specific period, prior to roasting and producing. If sent immediately for deactivation, the dried tea would retain the smell of fresh leaves and the color would be a little too dark and would look coarse.

The dried tea

The liquid

The brewed leaves

6. Machine-processed Long Jing tea variety

As the name indicates, this tea is processed with the help of machines; it is different from the traditional handmade Long Jing tea.

Tips

Through cooling and re-absorbing moisture, the deactivated leaves become invulnerable to crumbling.

The dried tea

The liquid

The brewed leaves

2. An Ji White Tea

A baked and roasted green tea variety, the white featherlike An Ji white tea is produced in Anji County of Zhejiang Province. In the 1980s, the mother tea bush was discovered in Daxi Village, Tianhuangping Town, Anji County. In the cool spring-time, the nearly opened buds of the tea bushes appear greenish, but soon turn white after opening fully. They are encased in two leaves. Subsequently, they turn green again. The vast plantations give an increasing yield each year.

Tips

The amino acid content in An Ji Bai white tea variety is 5–10.6%, twice or thrice as much as in the common green tea. The middle-brewing method is adopted this tea (refer to P109 for details): Moisten the dried tea once by steeping in a little hot water; shake the tea pot after the tea leaf floats on the water surface; brew.

The dried tea

The liquid

The brewed leaves

3. Zhejiang White Tea

In Zhejiang Province, some other areas outside Anji County also produce green tea processed from the fresh leaves of the white tea, but the taste does not match that of the An Ji white tea.

The dried tea

The liquid

The brewed leaves

4. An Ji Bai Pian

Also produced in Anji, this tea is naturally curved in appearance, deep green in color, with a lingering pleasant fragrance, refreshing taste and sweet aftertaste. The leaves settle at the bottom of the pot and the tea liquid is clear.

Tips

The fresh leaves of An Ji Pian and An Ji white tea are picked from different tea tree varieties.

The dried tea

The liquid

The brewed leaves

5. Organic Green Tea

Produced in Wuyi County of Zhenjiang Province, the organic green tea is mass produced. Its dried leaves are thin, deep green, with clear yellowish-green liquid, highly pleasant fragrance, rich and authentic taste and tender dark green brewed leaves.

The dried tea

The liquid

The brewed leaves

6. Organic Cui Jian Green Tea

Also produced in Wuyi County of Zhenjiang Province, the tea is a high-grade tender green tea, with a single-bud, jade green color of the dried tea, clear yellowish-green tea liquid, rich and lasting fragrance, mellow and refreshing taste and sweet aftertaste. The brewed leaves are tender and unbroken.

Brewing in a cup

The dried tea

The liquid

The brewed leaves

7. Kai Hua Long Ding

Also known as Da Long Cha, this tea is produced in Kaihua County of Zhejiang Province. It has a single bud, compact and erect contour and is jade green, has a refreshing and lasting fragrance, mellow and fresh taste, green and clear liquid and evenly brewed leaves.

The dried tea

The liquid

The brewed leaves

8. Xiangcha Tea

Produced in Songyang, Suichangand and some other counties of south Zhejiang, the tea has a compact curved appearance, deep green color, fragrance of chestnuts, mellow and refreshing taste, clear yellowish-green liquid and broken brewed leaves.

The dried tea

The liquid

The brewed leaves

II. Green Tea in Jiangsu Province

Well-known for its prominent landscape of rivers and lakes, Jiangsu Province boasts two tea production areas in the north and south, bifurcated by the Yangtze River. The main green tea plantations are Suzhou, Nanjing, Zhenjiang, Wuxi, Changshou and Yangzhou. The major famous tea are Dong Ting Bi Luo Chun, Nan Jing Yu Hua, Yang Xian Xue Ya, Li Yang Cui Bai, Wu Xi Hao Tea , Tai Hu Cui Zhu, Jing Tan, etc.

Tips

Yang Xian Xue Ya tea is named after Yangxian (present-day Yixing), where a historically famous tea brand was first created early in the Tang Dynasty (618–907).

Bi Luo Chun

There is a verse about the Bi Luo Chun tea: "All around the mountain grow tea bushes, the bluish-green and fragrant Bi Luo Chun tea, intoxicating a distance of 50km."

Commonly known as Xia Sha Ren Xiangwhich meaning "strikingly fragrant" in Chinese, this curled, spiral roasted green tea was named Bi Luo Chun by Emperor Kangxi of the Qing Dynasty. Originally produced in the eastern and western slopes of Mt. Dongting in Wu County of Jiangsu Province, it is long known for its "pretty appearance, tender color, rich fragrance and mellow taste." The dried tea is fine, curled and spiral, with silver fuzzy petiole. It has a rich and natural fragrance of flowers and fruits, a mellow taste and lingering aftertaste. The tea liquid is clear green, and the brewed leaves fine with tender buds.

Bi Luo Chun boasts a natural fragrance of flowers and fruits because the fresh leaves are picked from tea plantations with an abundance of fruits, such as pipa, apricot, prune, red bayberry, pearl, plum, pomegranate, chestnut, walnut, ginkgo, etc. There are four steps for processing this tea: (1) Spread the newly harvested leaves thinly on the ground to deactivate them; (2) roll and shape it; (3) when the tea has lost about 70% of its moisture content, knead softly into a round shape till the fuzzy petiole can be seen; and (4) desiccate it in the heated pan (completely dry the tea by spreading it on mulberry bark papers and baking together in the pan).

Bi Luo Chun tea roasting and producing involves skillful manual handling of the tea and continually processing the tea in the pans (roasting and rolling consecutively until it is completely dried).

Some other areas like Liyang City of Jinagsu Province also produce Bi Luo Chun tea; the color of the dried tea and fragrance is quite dissimilar. Other provinces like Guizhao and Jiangxi also produce a large quantity. Though some illegal tea traders may produce fake Bi Luo Chun by adding chlorophyll and pipa fuzz, the authentic variety can be discerned through a careful check of the color of the liquid, the brewing fragrance and the taste of the brewed liquid.

1. Dong Ting Bi Luo Chun

The authentic Bi Luo Chun tea is produced in the western Dongting Mountain of Suzhou City, Jiangsu Province.

The dried tea

The liquid

The brewed leaves

2. Li Yang Bi Luo Chun

The dried tea

The liquid

The brewed leaves

Tips

Guizhou Bi Luo Chun

The Guizhao Province also produces Bi Luo Chun, but the appearance and taste are significantly different from the original one.

The dried tea

The liquid

The brewed teaves

There are about 60,000–70,000 tender tea buds in every 500g Bi Luo Chun.

- Only fresh leaves with one bud and newly spread leaf is picked in keeping with the principle of "early picking, priority to tender buds and selection without impurities."

- For the middle-brewing method of Bi Luo Chun tea, the temperature of the boiled water should be around 75°.

- It is typical of the Bi Luo Chun tea plantation to plant fruits among tea bushes.

- Kneading into tiny round rolls is a critical procedure for "shaping white and greenish fuzz into curled, compact and fine dried tea."

- The various stories behind the renaming of the original Xia Sha Ren Xiang to Bi Luo Chun tea are: (1) It is curled and spiral. (2) The tea used to be processed in the Bi Luo nunnery with fresh tea leaves from the plantation at Bi Luo Mountain peak. (3) The name was given by Kang Xi, an emperor of the Qing Dynasty (1644–1911). It is said that there were clusters of tea bushes at the Bi Luo peak of the eastern Dongting Mountain, where local villagers often picked the fresh tea leaves and roasted them to make the Xia Sha Ren Xiang tea. Once, during his incognito travel to the south, Emperor Kang Xi was offered the Xia Sha Ren Xiang tea. After drinking the tea, the emperor was impressed by the special fragrance and taste. He thought its name too common to match its high quality, so the emperor renamed it "Bi Luo Chun" (literally "jade green spiral spring"). (4) According to legend a pretty and kind girl Bi Luo fell in love with a young fisherman, Ah Xiang. Unfortunately, an evil dragon wanted the girl as its concubine. To save her, Ah Xiang went to fight the dragon. By the end of the battle, Ah Xiang became unconscious from excessive bleeding. Frantic, Bi Luo climbed up the mountain to find some herbal medicine. She saw a cluster of tea bushes and picked the leaves to boil them. After drinking the soup, Ah Xiang recovered. Unfortunately, Bi Luo died from extreme exhaustion. Ah Xiang buried her under the tea bush. Surprisingly, thereafter, the tea bushes thrived, and this high-quality tea was named Bi Luo Chun to honor the girl.

Column 2

Quality
& Safety
Certification

The QS stamp is familiar for it is seen on the packaging of various foods and commodities, such as milk and yoghurt. The brands may vary but the stamp remains the same. What is QS? And what does QS certification mean?

QS is an acronym for "Quality Safety," adopted as a stamp of approval in China for food quality and safety administration. The products carrying a QS mark are deemed as conforming to mandatory tests by competent institutions of the country. Usually the production license code numbers are also printed, and only the foodstuffs with QS can be sold in the market. Since 2005, China General Administration of Quality Testing and Inspection officially put tea products in the category of foodstuffs and implemented the market-entry licensing system from 2006. So far many tea enterprises have successively gained the QS certification, and still others are applying for the certification.

For a long time, quality control of the tea industry was difficult because of the scattered tea plantations. As a result, it was difficult to segregate the conforming and nonconforming products, and pesticide residue and heavy metal content were above the minimum requirements for some tea varieties. Consequently, China's tea export volume decreased. In recent years, such incidents as the "toxin content in Bi Luo Chun" in Anhui Province and dyed "Bi Luo Chun" in Guizhou Province have had a negative impact. Therefore, quality and safety administration in the tea industry have become an important issue. Enforcement of QS certification ensures safe tea products in the market.

Quality Safety

III. Green Tea in Anhui Province

Anhui Province covers two major tea productions areas. Southern Anhui falls to the south of the Yangtze River tea production area while Northern Anhui belongs to the north of the Yangtze tea production area. Tea plantations are mainly distributed in the Huangshan, Jiuhuashan, Dabieshan and some other mountains. According to *the Annals of Huizhou Prefecture* (present-day North Anhui Province), the tea plantation in Mt. Huangshan started in the Song Dynasty, and then thrived in the Ming Dynasty. Today, the famous green tea brands include Huang Shan Mao Feng Tea, Tai Ping Hou Kui Tea, Yong Xi Huo Qing Tea, etc.

1. Huang Shan Mao Feng

Cloudy and misty Mt. Huangshan's miraculous power breeds Mao Feng tea. The red-crowned fuzzy petiole is brilliant, the fragrance strong even after three brews.

Orchid-shaped, Shan Mao Feng Huang is a brand of baked green tea. Hailed as the best of Mao Feng tea, Huang Shan Mao Feng has a sparrow-tongue-like shape, silvery white fuzz, golden liquid, refreshingly mellow and sweet taste, and the brewed leaves are tender yellow. The impurities are picked out before processing. The processing involves deactivation, followed by rolling and desiccation. Traditionally, desiccation is the "primary drying" over hot charcoal and the "complete drying" over less hot charcoal. Modern processing involves desiccating machines. The quality is characterized by a smooth, yellowish-green color similar to ivory, golden-fish leaves, fat and average buds, clear rich and lasting fragrance, refreshingly mellow taste and a sweet aftertaste, clear and bright liquid, and tender yellow brewed leaves.

There is a wonderful legend about Huang Shan Mao Feng Tea. Long ago, there lived a girl called Luo Xiang. Her beauty earned her the name "a phoenix in remote mountains." She had many suitors. The girl decided to choose her ideal husband through the magic of tea.

Shi Yong, the man she loved, was able to win her. But as revenge, some villainous people beat Shi Yong to death. The heartbroken Luo Xiang asked her people to move Shi Yong's body beneath a tea bush beside a mountain brook. She watered the tea bush with her own blood and tears. At last, the heavenly gods, touched by her deeds, made Shi Yong rise from death by nurturing him with the tea leaves of the bush above him. The two lovers were happily reunited and the tea bush became the origin of Huang Shan Mao Feng.

1. Machine-processed Huang Shan Mao Feng

The dried tea

The liquid

The brewed leaves

2. Manually processed Huang Shan Mao Feng

Tips

To brew Huang Shan Mao Feng, apply the middle-brewing method (refer to P109 for details). At the beginning tea leaves may float on the surface but gradually they will sink to the bottom of the teapot or are suspended in the liquid. The brewed leaves resemble the blooming orchids, pleasing to watch.

The dried tea

The liquid

The brewed leaves

2. Tai Ping Hou Kui

The tea is a type of baked green tea produced around Houkeng, Houcun and Hougang in Taiping County, Huangshan City, Anhui Province. While brewing, the dried leaves bloom into full leaves and buds displaying a dark red central vein. The harvesting is relatively late, usually beginning around the Grain Rain (20th day of the 4th month of the lunar year). The processing involves deactivation and desiccation. The deactivated leaves are spread on bamboo sheets and baked in baking baskets, (the primary baking); after 60–70% of the moisture content is lost, the leaves are removed from the baskets and spread for cooling for approximately 2 hours. They are again baked in the baskets till 80–90% of the moisture content is lost, then cooled once again. Finally, it is baked completely dry. The Tai Ping Hou Kui Tea features a straight and heavy appearance with two sides of the leaves embracing one hidden bud, gray-green color, rich fuzz, strong and lasting fragrance, mellow taste and sweet aftertaste, verdurous liquid and evenly settled bright tea leaves.

1. Manually processed Tai Ping Hou Kui tea

The liquid

The brewed leaves

The dried tea

2. Machine-processed Tai Ping Hou Kui tea

The dried tea　　　　　The liquid　　　　　The brewed tea

According to legend, long ago, there lived an old white monkey couple in Mt. Huangshan. One day, one of their sons was lost. Searching for him, they became exhausted and fell down in the mountains. Wang Lao'er, found them and brought them home. He cured them with herbs. The couple was so grateful that they decided to stay and help Wang Lao'er. The tea produced here was called Hou tea (literally "Monkey tea") or Hou Jian tea ("Monkey tea buds"). The quality of the tea was excellent, especially the variety processed by Wang Lao'er. It was distinguished as Hou Kui tea or Kui Jian (literally *Kui* meaning "champion") for its superior quality.

Tai Ping Hou Kui tea has three grades: Hou Kui, Hou Jian and Jian Cha.

To brew Tai Ping Hou Kui, apply the middle- or bottom-brewing method. Porcelain cups work better. The tea leaves are long. Deep cups are preferred.

Tips

The tea is characterized by high fragrance in the first brew, strong taste in the second brew and light fragrance in the third and fourth brews.

3. Liu An Gua Pian

Processed from a single leaf without stem and bud, Liu An Gua Pian tea is produced in Liu'an, Jingzhai and Huoshan of Anhui Province. Though the yield is more in Liu'an County, the quality is better in Jingshan County. The tea features a blackish-green melon-seed-shaped singular leaf and hoarfrost-like-coated leaf surface. The tea liquid is dark green with a lingering fruity fragrance and mellow taste with a sweet aftertaste. Baking this tea is the most distinctive of its kind; it is baked three times.

The dried tea · The liquid · The brewed leaves

↑ High-quality Liu An Gua Pian Tea

The dried tea · The liquid · The brewed leaves

↑ Common Liu An Gua Pian Tea

4. Song Luo Cha

The historically famous Song Luo Tea is produced in Mt. Songluo of Xiuning County, Anhui Province. Ancient medicinal literature records that the Song Luo Tea can be used as a medicinal herb for facilitating digestion, relief of internal heat and balancing of the *qi* (vital energy). The bright green compactly curled tea has a strong taste, refreshing fragrance, bright green liquid, tender and green brewed leaves. According to folklore, during the Ming Dynasty, when typhus and diarrhea were epidemic in Xiuning, locals burned incense and worshiped the Buddha in the Rangfu Temple. The Abbot sent every worshipper a pack of Song Luo Tea in return. He told the less-serious patients to brew the tea in hot water, while the more serious ones were to mix the tea with raw ginger, salt and glutinous rice, roast the mixture till brown, mash the roasted tea and drink it with some water. All the patients recovered quickly.

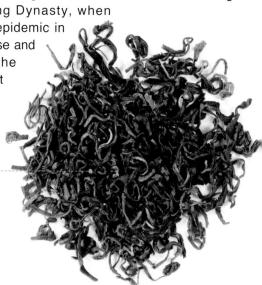

The dried tea

The liquid

The brewed leaves

IV. Green Tea in Sichuan Province

Located in southwest China, Sichuan Province is in the original tea belt. Mostly, tea plantations are developed across mountain ranges in Yibin, Emeishan, Zigong, Ya'an, Qionglai, and Suining. The major tea brands include Meng Ding Gan Lu Tea, Meng Ding Shi Hua, E Mei Zhu Ye Qing, Wen Jun Lv Cha, Meng Shan Que She, Qing Cheng Xue Ya Tea.

1. E Mei Zhu Ye Qing tea

The flat E Mei Zhu Ye Qing tea was developed in the 1960s, when Chen Yi (1901–1972), a communist general, statesman and a marshal of the PLA, visited Mt. Emei. He drank a cup of this tea and praised its delicate fragrance and sweet and mellow aftertaste. The Marshal named it Zhu Ye Qing (literally "bamboo leaf green") because the tea resembled tender bamboo leaves.

The tea is green, flat, smooth and straight. The liquid is bright green, light but with lingering fragrance, refreshing and mellow taste, unbroken and clear brewed leaves.

The leaves float on the surface of the water initially, and after absorbing moisture, gradually sink to the bottom. The most suitable teapot is the common transparent glass cup. The middle-brewing method is adopted for this tea. The best way to enjoy this tea is to observe the dance of the tea leaves, smell the fragrance, appreciate the delicate fragrance of the tea and slowly sip the tea.

Brewing in cups

(E Mei Zhu Ye Qing)
The dried tea

The liquid

The brewed leaves

2. Meng Ding Gan Lu

"The water in the center of the Yangtze River is the best, while the tea on the top of Mt. Mengding is ranked first."

The curved Meng Ding Gang Lu is a brand of green tea produced in Mt. Mengding in the western Mingshan County of Sichuan Province. It is said that Wu Lizheng, known as the "Forefather of Tea" and the "Master of Dew," personally planted seven tea bushes in the Shangqing Peak that are still seen today. In addition this area also produces the yellow tea Meng Ding Huang Ya.

The Meng Ding Gang Lu features curled leaves, fuzzy buds, bright yellowish-green liquid, mild fragrance, refreshingly sweet taste, and yellowish-green and tender brewed leaves. To brew the tea, the middle-brewing method should be adopted (see details P109). The fine and tender buds sink to the bottom and then unfurl after absorbing moisture.

The dried tea

The liquid

The brewed leaves

V. Green Tea in Henan Province

Located in the tea production area of the north Yangtze River, production is mainly concentrated in the counties of Huangchuan, Luoshan, Guangshan, Guchi, Shangcheng, Tongwu and Miyang of Xinyang Prefecture. In its long history, it is recorded that the tea plant was grown as early as 1,200 years ago. The best-known green tea brand is Xin Yang Mao Jian Tea from Xinyang County while other famous brands include Yun Ya Cui Hao, Yang Tian Xue Lv, Jing Gang Bi Lv and Tai Bai Yin Feng in Huangchan, Guchi, Shangcheng and Tongwu counties, respectively.

Xin Yang Mao Jian

Xin Yang Mao Jian tea is produced in Xinyang City of Henan Province, where the top-quality tea plantations of "five *Yun*s (clouds) and two *Tang*s (ponds)" are located. The "five *Yun*s" refer to the five mountains: Mt. Cheyun, Tianyun, Yunwu, Jiyun and Liangyun, while the "two *Tang*s," are Heilongtang and Bailongtang.

The tea is compact, fine and round , fuzzy, jade green in color, clear liquid, strong and lasting fragrance, refreshingly mellow and sweet taste and aftertaste and tender and green brewed leaves.

The dried tea   The liquid   The brewed l

↑ High-quality Xin Yang Mao Jian Tea

The dried tea · The liquid · The brewed leaves

↑ Medium-quality Xin Yang Mao Jian Tea

The dried tea · The liquid · The brewed leaves

↑ Common Xin Yang Mao Jian Tea

Tips

The Xinyang Tea Culture Festival (April 2006) auctioned the Liang Tian Yu Ye tea of the green tea brand Xin Yang Mao Jian at a whopping price of RMB149,000 yuan for merely 100g of the tea.

Xin Yang Mao Jian Tea was awarded the gold prize in the 1915 Panama Pacific International Exposition.

To brew Xin Yang Mao Jian Tea, adopt the middle-brewing method use glass cups or porcelain teapots.

VI. Green Tea in Jiangxi Province

Jiangxi Province is in the tea production area south of the Yangtze River. The tea plantations are mainly distributed among mountains ranges, such as Jinggang, Lushan, Dazhang and Jiuling. The tea is also produced in the counties of Wuyuan, Ningdu, Xiushui, Shangyou and Nanchang. The province mainly produces green tea. The major brands include Lu Shan Yun Wu Tea, Wu Yuan Ming Mei Tea, Xiao Bu Yan Tea, Shuang Jian Green Tea, Gou Gu Nao Tea, Shang Rao Bai Meng Tea.

1. Wu Yuan Ming Mei

There is a popular saying: "Where can Ming Mei Tea be found? In the households of the most beautiful countryside!" Wu Yuan Ming Mei Tea is produced in the Wuyuan County of Jiangxi Province, with the reputation of the "Most Beautiful Countryside in China." Situated along the border between Anhui and Jiangxi Province, Wuyuan was under the administration of the Hui Prefecture in the past.

In March 2005, the local government applied for registration of a trade mark known as "Wuyuan Green Tea." Wu Yuan Ming Mei Tea, the most famous green tea in Wuyuan, is a semi-baked and semi-roasted green tea variety processed through deactivation, rolling, baking, roasting in pans and rebaking.

It is curved like eyebrows, with brilliant white fuzz, refreshing, sweet and mellow taste, lasting fruity fragrance. The tea liquid is green, with tender, even and unbroken brewed leaves.

To brew, adopt the tea middle-brewing method. While steeping, the leaves resemble "falling plum blossoms." The fragrance and taste are best in the second brew, and the taste and fragrance remain even after several brews.

The dried tea   The liquid   The brewed leaves

↑ High-quality Wu Yuan Ming Mei Tea

The dried tea   The liquid   The brewed leaves

↑ Common Wu Yuan Ming Mei Tea

2. Wu Yuan Green Tea

Simply called Wu Lv, it is the staple green tea of average quality produced in Wuyuan. The tea has high fragrance, mellow taste, clear liquid and green brewed leaves. Produced long ago mainly for export, it has now a famous brand.

The dried tea

The liquid

The brewed leaves

3. De Yu Huo Cha

Produced around Wuyuan County, this tea is straight, bright green with white fuzz, has a sweet and mellow taste, strong and lasting fragrance, yellowish-green liquid and unbroken brewed leaves.

The dried tea

The liquid

The brewed leaves

VII. Green Tea in Hunan Province

Located south of the Yangtze River, Hunan Province is one of the major green tea production areas in China. Major tea plantations are in cities or prefectures such as Changsha, Changde, Henyang, Yueyang, Yiyang and Binzhou. Famous tea brands in the province include Gao Qiao Yin Feng, Xiang Bo Lv, An Hua Song Zhen, Dong Ting Chun Ya, Lan Ling Mao Jian , Gui Dong Ling Long, Nan Yue Yun Wu, Jiang Hua Gu Cha, Zi Xing Gou Nao Tribute Tea, Tao Yuan Wild Tea and Jie Tan Cha. The green tea in Hunan is rich in element composition, and has a strong and refreshing taste.

Hunan Tea Production Area

1. Gao Qiao Yin Feng Tea

The curved Gao Qiao Yin Feng is a brand of baked green tea developed by the Tea Research Institute of Hunan Province in 1959, and produced in Gaoqiao Tow, Changsha County. It features a compact, slim and curved appearance with silver white fuzz, jade green color, bright yellowish-green liquid, strong and lasting fragrance, refreshing and mellow taste, tender, evenly brewed leaves.

The dried tea

The liquid

The brewed leaves

2. Shi Men Yin Feng Tea

The curved Shi Men Yin Feng is a brand of baked green tea produced in Shimen County in west Hunan Province. It is characterized by white fuzz, bright yellowish-green liquid, strong and lasting fragrance, refreshingly mellow taste with sweet aftertaste and verdant, even and unbroken brewed leaves.

The dried tea

The liquid

The brewed leaves

3. Xiang Bo Lv Tea

The tea is developed by the Tea Research Institute of Hunan Province and produced around Gaoqiao Town. It is characterized by a curved appearance, green color, bright yellowish-green liquid, pure and authentic chestnut fragrance, refreshing and mellow taste, and tender and soft brewed leaves.

The dried tea

The liquid

The brewed leaves

Column 3 Green Tea Storage

The early spring green tea is the best in quality. It has a bright green color, strong and lasting fragrance, green, bright and clear liquid and a refreshing taste.

Storage is critical for green tea quality. Its deterioration leads to its color to change from green and bright to withered yellow, the liquid turns darkish yellow, losing fragrance and taste becoming bland. Absorption of foreign odors may greatly affect the quality. Therefore, it is important to learn how to store it.

Factors contributing to deterioration of green tea

Temperature

Temperature is a major factor causing deterioration. Higher the temperature, faster will be the oxidization of the tea polyphenol, and consequently, quicker the deterioration.

Oxygen

Elements such as tea polyphenol in a tea leaf may be oxidized in conditions having around 20% oxygen in the air. Generally, the degree of deterioration is directly proportionally to the duration of its contact with the air.

Moisture

Tea is a hydrophilic substance; therefore the moisture content in a tea leaf will also increase when stored in a place with high moisture. Many elements contained in a tea leaf are hydrophilic compounds which may cause molding and accelerate deterioration.

Light

Due to photosynthesis, pigments and esters contained in a tea leaf may produce some foreign odors.

Foreign odors

Tea has a porous texture liable to absorb odors and consequently, cause deterioration if the tea is stored in an environment having varied unpleasant odors.

Storage at low temperature

Green tea can be stored in a refrigerator. (1) Pack the tea in small packs; (2) Seal the tea packs and store in temperatures of 3–6°C. (Note: The tea should be sealed and preferably stored separately to avoid absorption of foreign odors. If possible, keep in a refrigerator especially for tea storage.) Take out the tea leaves for drinking. Keep outside till the temperature of tea equals room temperature.

Storage in sealed packs at normal temperature

The green tea can be put in sealed packs and stored in a cool, dry place at normal temperature. The tea packs must be sealed, airtight and away from light, moisture and foreign odors.

Storage after deoxidation

Green tea cannot be vacuum-packed because it may break the dried tea, and consequently, affect the appearance which is critical to the quality. However, deoxidizer placement and nitrogen-filling ways of deoxidation can be adopted for green tea storage.

Storage with dry lime

Pack the tea in air-permeable papers. Keep dried lime in a cloth bag and place at the center inside the pottery jar. Put the tea around the bag, and finally place the jar in a cool and dry place. Check the lime regularly and replace when it is found to be moisturized. This is the traditional way to store Long Jing tea.

The principle of green tea storage is "low temperature and moisture and avoidance of light, oxygen and foreign odors." However, the tea bought home must contain 6% moisture, otherwise it deteriorates. In case of large quantities, it must be packed in small units for the convenience of drinking or storage. Furthermore, it is recommended that the same package be used for the same variety and quality tea otherwise the quality may be affected.

VIII. Green Tea in Shandong Province

Located on the north bank of the lower reaches of the Yangtze River, Shandong Province is in the north Yangtze River tea production area. Generally considered non-tea-producing province, in fact, tea production started in the 1970s. Today, the tea production areas are Laoshan, Rizhao and Chunanyimeng. The famous tea brands include Lao Shan Green Tea and Ri Zhao Green Tea.The high-quality spring tea, characterized by strong taste, pure and clean liquid and lasting aftertaste, is typically Ri Zhao Green Tea.

Lao Shan Green Tea

Lao Shan Green Tea is a typical brand of semi-baked and semi-roasted green tea produced in the Mt. Laoshan range in Shandong Province. The tea leaves are neat and curled, deep green in color; bright yellowish-green liquid, strong chestnut fragrance, mellow taste with sweet aftertaste, and tender, soft, even and unbroken brewed leaves.

The liquid

The brewed leaves

The dried tea

IX. Green Tea in Guizhou Province

Located in the Yunnan-Guizhou Plateau of southwest China, Guizhou Province is in the southwest tea production area. The green tea is produced in the counties or cities of Meitan, Liping, Shuicheng, Liupanshui, Guiding, Guiyang, Luodian, Duoyun and Fenggang in the province. The famous tea brands include Du Yun Mao Jian, Zun Yi Mao Feng, Guiding Yun Wu, Dong Po Mao Jian, and Feng Gang Fu Xi.

1. Mei Tan Que She

This baked green tea is produced in Meitan County, Guizhou Province. The leaves are flat and smooth, bright green in color, mild and clean liquid, a mild fragrance, refreshing and sweet taste and fine, tender and unbroken brewed leaves.

The liquid

The brewed leaves

The dried tea

2. Mei Tan Cui Ya

Also produced in Meitan County, the tea features a flat appearance, green with sharp contours, mild and lingering fragrance, bright green liquid, refreshing, sweet and mellow taste, and even and unbroken brewed leaves.

The dried tea

The liquid

The brewed leaves

3. Du Yun Mao Jian Tea

The tea is a historically famous brand of curved spiral tea variety. It is also known as "Fishhook Tea" because of its shape. The tea leaves are curved with white fuzz, bright yellowish-green liquid, strong and lasting fragrance, refreshing and heavy taste, refreshing and sweet aftertaste, and yellowish-green and bright brewed leaves.

The dried tea

The liquid

The brewed leaves

4. Zun Yi Mao Feng

This straight-lined tea variety is produced in Meitan County. It is named after the Zunyi Conference, a historic event of the CPC in January 1935. It features a compact, fine and round appearance covered with white fuzz, bright yellowish-green liquid, mild and lasting fragrance, strong, mellow and refreshing taste and green brewed leaves.

The dried tea

The liquid

The brewed leaves

X. Green Tea in Shaanxi Province

Located in cold northwest China, Shaanxi Province is in the north Yangtze River tea production area. The cold climate is not conducive for tea production. However, in south Shaanxi, close to Sichuan and Hubei provinces, known as "little Jiangnan" is a small area similar to the temperate and fertile area south of the Yangtze River. Ziyang boasts a long history of tea production (Ba Shu tea was produced before the Tang Dynasty). It is a mountainous county rich in selenium content—a trace element essential to our health, to strengthen the immunologic function in the body. Therefore, Fu Xi Tea (literally "selenium-rich tea") produced in the county is also known as a tonic tea. The famous tea brands include Wu Zi Green Tea, Wu Zi Xian Hao Tea, etc.

1. Wu Zi Green Tea

The tea is produced in Xixiang County, Shaanxi Province. Its leaves are neat and compact,deep green in color, with bright greenish-yellow liquid, fragrance of chestnuts, strong and heavy taste, and yellowish green brewed leaves, with rich natural content of zinc and selenium.

The dried tea   The liquid   The brewed leaves

2. Wu Zi Xian Hao

The tea is produced in Mt. Wuzi in Xixiang County, Shaanxi Province. It has a flat and smooth appearance, is jade green in color with white fuzz, bright green liquid, lasting fragrance of orchids, mellow and heavy taste with a refreshing and sweet aftertaste, tender and evenly settled brewed leaves, and rich natural content of zinc and selenium.

The dried tea

The liquid

The brewed leaves

3. Zi Yang Mao Jian

The tea is produced in Mt. Qinling in Ziyang County, Shaanxi Province. Its leaves are curled, round and compact, jade green in color with white fuzz, bright green liquid, mild and lasting fragrance, and refreshing and mellow taste with a sweet aftertaste. The area produces a green tea rich in selenium content in addition to its general green tea properties.

The dried tea

The liquid

The brewed leaves

4. Zi Yang Cui Feng Tea

This tea is produced in the depths of the Mt. Qinling range of Ziyang County, Shaanxi Province. Its jade green leaves are flat and straight with fat and sturdy buds, white fuzz, clear green liquid, lasting fragrance, mellow and refreshing taste and tender and evenly settled brewed leaves.

The dried tea   The liquid

The brewed leaves

5. Fu Xi Tea (Se-enriched Tea)

This tea is a brand of staple green tea variety produced in Ziyang County.

The dried tea   The liquid

The brewed leaves

Fu Xi Tea Varieties

Fu Xi Tea is rich in selenium content in comparison with general tea varieties, such as Wu Zi Xian Hao Tea, Zi Yang Mao Jian Tea, and Zi Yang Yin Zhen Tea.

Selenium, discovered early in 1817, was considered to be a hazardous element. However, in 1973, the World Health Organization declared selenium to be a trace element essential to the human body.

There are two types of selenium—inorganic or organic. The former is found in soil and minerals while the later in fauna and flora. Approximately 15–30% of selenium can be dissolved in the tea liquid while brewing.

Selenium helps strengthen immunity and prevent synthetization of ammonium.It proves effective for antitumorigenesis, antioxidation, purifying free radicals, deferring senility and recovering from radiation damage. Furthermore, selenium can also detoxify hazardous elements through excretion to protect skin and prevent cancer.

Today, Fu Xi tea is mainly produced in Enshi City of Hubei Province, Ziyang County of Shaanxi, Fenggang County of Guizhou and Shitai County of Anhui in China.

Fu Xi tea from Guizhou

Zi Yang Mao Jian Tea from Shaanxi

Zi Yang Yin Zhen Tea from Shaanxi

XI. Green Tea in the Guangxi Region

Located in south China, Guangxi Zhuang Autonomous Region is in the south China tea production area. The long history of its tea plantation is recorded in the *Classic of Tea* by Lu Yu of the Tang Dynasty. Tea plantations in the region are mainly in Guiping, Lingping, Guilin, Zhaoping, Lingshan and Wuzhou. The major brands include Gui Ping Xi Shan Cha, Nan Shan Bai Mao Cha, Gui Lin Mao Jian, Ling Yun Bai Hao, etc.

1. Ling Luo Chun

Produced in Lingyun County of Guangxi Zhuang Autonomous Region, the jade green tea has a curled appearance with white fuzz, clear bright, yellowish-green liquid, a fragrance of chestnut, strong and heavy taste, and green brewed leaves.

The dried tea

The liquid

The brewed leaves

2. Ling Yun Bai Hao

Produced in Lingyun County of Guangxi Zhuang Autonomous Region, the silver gray tea is characterized by its sturdy appearance with white fuzz, strong and lasting fragrance, clear jade green liquid and green brewed leaves.

The dried tea

The liquid

The brewed leaves

XII. Green Tea in Yunnan Province

Located in the southwest China tea production area, Yunnan is one of the original places of tea plantation. It is the most concentrated production base of the well-known Puer tea. Most tea plantations are found in the prefectures of Pu'er, Xishuangbanna, Lincang and Baoshan. The major green tea brands include Nan Nuo Bai Hao Tea, Ding Qing Tea, Yi Liang Bao Hong Cha Tea, etc.

1. Dian Qing Tea

The tea is a sun-dried green tea produced in Yunnan Province. Mostly used as raw material for processing Pu-erh tea, a small amount is directly brewed. Its dried leaves are loose, naturally bent, with sturdy buds, dark green color, a distinctive smell of the sun, bright yellowish-green liquid, mellow, refreshing and strong taste with sweet aftertaste, and yellowish-green and unbroken brewed leaves.

The liquid

The brewed leaves

The dried tea

2. Yu Luo Tea

The tea is a spiral-shaped variety processed from fresh leaves of the big-leaf tea-plants in Xishuangbanna. It features a silvery green appearance with white fuzz, sturdy and fat buds, strong fragrance, bright yellowish-green liquid, mellow and refreshing taste with sweet aftertaste and enduring brews.

The dried tea

The liquid

The brewed leaves

Column 5 Green Tea in Japan

Most brands of Japanese green tea, such as Sencha, Gyokuro and Tencha, are green tea processed by steam deactivation. Steamed green tea is characterized by green—green liquid and green tea brewed leaves.

Sencha Tea

This tea is a brand of steamed tea produced in Japan. It features tightly knotted appearance, deep green color, tender buds, jade green liquid, refreshing taste with broken green brewed leaves.

The dried tea   The liquid

The brewed leaves

Sencha Tea Powder

This tea features tightly knotted appearance, bright green color, unclear green liquid, refreshing taste and broken green brewed leaves.

Tips

Sencha Tea powder is a combination of Sencha Tea and its powder; therefore the tea liquid is green and unclear due to the powder suspension in the liquid.

The dried tea   The liquid

The brewed leaves

Tea Powder

The tea is a brand of steamed green tea processed by mashing the dried tea into a fine tea powder of specific particle sizes, usually above 300 um. (Um is a commonly used unit for particle size measurement).

The liquid

Tea powder

Grinder for tea powder

Other Green Tea in Japan

↑ Sencha Tea

↑ Genmaicha Tea

↑ Sencha Tea

↑ Kukicha Tea

Reprocessed Green Tea

Part 3

Many people know of jasmine tea. But, not everyone knows that jasmine tea is a type of green tea. Then how is green tea processed into jasmine tea? This part introduces the different types of teas, including jasmine tea, that are made from the basic green tea.

I. Scented Tea

Scented tea is reprocessed green tea from baked base tea or roasted tea and the fresh nearly blooming flower buds as raw materials. Usually jasmine or other flowers, such as magnolia, bitter orange flower, chloranthus and gardenia are selected for adding fragrance.

A little gardenia optimizes scenting jasmine tea. However, too much gardenia will make "the fragrance of gardenia strong." It is normal to find some gardenia petals in the dried jasmine-scented tea. The quality of the scented tea depends on the quality of the base tea, the flower and the scenting technique.

The scenting process of jasmine tea is comparatively complicated. First, pick the jasmine flower and prepare the tea base; secondly, select the nearly bloomed flowers, mix them with the tea base for static scenting; after the initial scenting, sift out the flowers and bake the tea leaf till it becomes dry. "Extracting flowers" is scenting with a small amount of top-quality fresh flowers and packing to store the scented tea. Only fresh flowers are used for every scenting of tea of high quality, while for lower grades, flowers are reused.

The quality of jasmine-scented tea produced in Fujian is better than that in Guangxi, Yunnan, Chongqing, Sichuan, Hunan and other provinces.

Scented tea has a strong, fresh and lasting fragrance. It is mellow and refreshing in taste, with clean bright liquid.

Scented tea varieties are mainly sold to north China, northeast China, Sichuan (particularly Chengdu City), and some of it is exported to Japan, Southeast Asia, western Europe and beyond.

1. Jasmine Yin Zhen

Produced in east Fujian Province, the tea is needle-shaped, with white fuzz, clear yellowish-green liquid, fresh, strong and lasting fragrance, refreshing taste, and yellowish-green and tender brewed leaves.

The dried tea

The liquid

The brewed leaves

2. Jasmine Long Zhu

Also produced in east Fujian, the tea is pearllike with white fuzz, bright yellowish-green liquid, pure, authentic, strong, high and lasting mixed fragrance of jasmine and green tea, strong and heavy taste, and yellowish-green and slightly tender brewed leaves. The taste is usually stronger than that of Jasmine Yin Zhen scented tea.

The dried tea

The liquid

The brewed leaves

3. Bi Tan Piao Xue

Produced in the area of Mt. Mengding, the tea is compact, fine, and curved, with a few dried jasmine flowers. The liquid is bright greenish-yellow, fresh, strong and with lasting fragrance. It is refreshing and mellow in taste, endures brew, and has tender and evenly settled brewed leaves.

The dried tea

The liquid

The brewed leaves

4. Jasmine Nv Er Huan

Also produced in east Fujian, the tea is a brand of organic jasmine scented tea. It is circular in shape, with white fuzz, bright yellowish-green liquid, pure and authentic fragrance, strong, heavy and refreshing taste and tender and soft brewed leaves with buds partly wrapped within the leaves.

The dried tea

The liquid

The brewed leaves

5. Jasmine Jin Sui

Also produced in east Fujian, the wheat ear-shaped tea has white fuzz, bright yellowish-green liquid, high and lasting fragrance, mellow, authentic, sweet and refreshing taste and yellowish-green, even and unbroken brewed leaves.

The dried tea

The liquid

The brewed leaves

6. Organic Yu Ya

The organic tea is produced in Heng County of Guangxi Zhuang Autonomous Region. It features a single-bud-shaped appearance, even, unbroken white fuzz, clear yellowish-green liquid, strong flowery fragrance, refreshing taste and sweet aftertaste and yellowish-green, tender and soft brewed leaves.

The dried tea

The liquid

The brewed leaves

7. Organic Scented Tea

The tea is a variety of staple organic scented tea produced in Xi County of Anhui Province. It is curved, brownish-green in color, tea leaves contain dried flower, yellowish-green liquid, pure and authentic fragrance, strong taste and yellowish-green and less bright brewed leaves.

The dried tea

The liquid

The brewed leaves

Column 6  Jasmine Tea

"Jasmine has no beauty to behold, but its faint scent excels all the other autumn flowers."

Jasmine is a genus of vines in the oleaceae family. Originally grown in ancient India, it was transplanted into China 1,700 years ago. First planted in Yunnan, it was widely distributed to Guangdong, Fujian, Guangxi, Jiangsu, Zhejiang, Anhui, Hunan, Hubei and Sichuan. Today, the flowers are mainly used for scenting jasmine tea. There are also some jasmine plantations in north China, mostly as an ornamental plant. Jasmine is a thermophilic plant and should be protected in a greenhouse.

The flowers, blooming from April through September, are categorized into three groups: spring, midsummer and autumn. Spring flowers harvested before the first quarter of July are also known as "plum blossoms"; they feature the poorest quality for scenting tea because of their small size and light fragrance. Midsummer flowers, harvested from the middle of July to the third quarter of August, are the best quality. And those that are harvested in the third quarter of August are called autumn jasmine flowers; the quality stands second after the midsummer.

Today, jasmine is planted in Yunjiang and Changning counties of Yunnan Province, Heng County of Guangxi Region and Zhenghe County of Fujian Province.

Dried jasmine flowers are usually used for traditional Chinese medicine. Taken after meals, they have curative effects, such as aiding digestion, balancing vital energy and soothing the nerves, eliminating depression, relieving emotional tension, and other discomforts (e.g. fatigue, headache). In addition, the flowers are also made into fragrant packs or applied for showering, hair-washing and skin care.

Simple jasmine drink

Raw materials: 2–3g dried jasmine flowers
A small amount of sugar and honey.
Brewing: Brew the flowers in hot water for 2–3 minutes, and add sugar and honey. Your drink is ready.

Jasmine flowers

II. Compressed Green Tea

Compressed green tea is a variety of green tea produced through direct compression of the rolled tea leaves. They are molded into various shapes for desiccation. Primarily processed tea leaves are streamed into soft tea leaves and then re-compressed with molds into various shapes to be desiccated. This includes Tuo Cha Green Tea and newly compressed raw Puer Cake. The tea can be easily transported and stored. The various molded patterns on the compressed tea products add to its ornamental value.

Tuo Cha Green Tea

Tea used for decoration

Qi Zi Bing Cha Green Tea

III. Green Tea Extract

Also known as Instantly Soluble Green Tea, green tea extract is a process by which soluble elements contained in the tea are extracted by brewing in hot water and then condensed and dried into granular particles or powder. Free from tea dregs, it can be brewed in cool water or had together with fruit juice or foods.

1. Tea polyphenols tablets

Also known as Catechin, these tablets are a new and high-tech healthy food made from extracted polyphenols in the tea. Powder, capsule or granular tea polyphenols tablets have curative effects such as eliminating free radicals, reducing inflammation, disinfection, deferring senility, hypolipidemic, preventing cardiovascular diseases and strengthening immune function.

Tea polyphenols tablets

2. Instantly Soluble Tea Powder

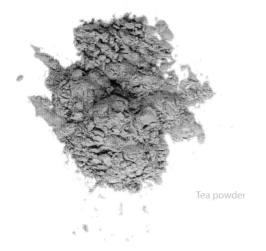

Tea powder

The brewed liquid

IV. Green Tea Bags

Also know as "Green Tea Pack," the tea is packaged in filter paper in unilocular or bilocular bags.

To brew, the portable pack is directly placed in a teapot, making its use convenient for office-goers.

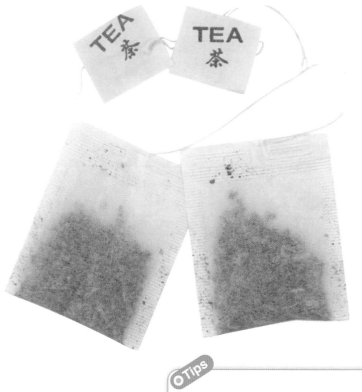

Tips

Keep the brewed green tea bags in a refrigerator to use for relieving eye fatigue. Do not use newly brewed particles because they can scorch the skin.

V. Beverages and Foods Containing Green Tea

Green tea beverages, tea wine, melon seeds, desserts and chewing gum may contain green tea extracts.

Tips

Green tea is also used in daily health products, such as toothpaste, face wash and shampoo.

Column 7 Ku Ding Tea

Also known as Fu Ding Tea or Gao Lu Tea, Ku Ding Tea is a traditional "half-tea" processed with the leaves of Kuding (*Aquifoliaceae Ilex latifolia*) tea-plants through the normal tea processing technique. Kuding tea-plants can be found in Guangdong, Fujian, Guangxi, Hainan, Zhejiang, Hunan and Jiangxi. Although known as a "half-tea," Ku Ding Tea's history as a traditional health drink is more than 2,000 years old. It was even revered as "tea of ceremonies" in the Han Dynasty. The tea has a fresh fragrance, bitter taste followed by sweet aftertaste, clean and yellowish-green liquid, mellow and strong taste and enduring brew. It can relieve heat, reduce inflammation, detoxify, prevent cardiac and diuretic diseases, control of high blood pressure and help weight loss.

Small-leaf Ku Ding Tea

The dried tea

The liquid

The brewed leaves

Ku Ding Tea has two categories: large-leaf Ku Ding Tea processed with the leaves from the Ku Ding tea plants of *arbor aquifoliaceae genus* in the hollyllex family. The tea is made only from the singular spiral tea leaves; the other is small-leaf Ku Ding Tea processed from Ku Ding tea-plants belonging to the *clusiaceae genus*. The tea is fine, deep green, giving a jade green liquid. Its brewing is described as "verdant hills and green waters" or "beautiful hills and clear waters."

Brewing Ku Ding Tea is the same as other green tea varieties. The amount of dried tea is a half stick of large-leaf Ku Ding or 1–2g small-leaf Ku Ding for every 150ml water; steep for 1–2 minutes.

Large-leaf Ku Ding Tea

The dried tea

The liquid

The brewed leaves

Brewing Fragrant Green Tea

Part 4

Making a good cup of green tea requires some knowledge. Different types of green tea require different water temperatures. Did you know there are three methods for brewing green tea, namely the "top brewing", "middle brewing" and "bottom brewing" methods. This part shows us how to make a simple cup of green tea as well as gives detailed instructions on brewing a few typical green teas.

I. Six Key Factors for Brewing Green Tea

Usually, an excellent cup (pot) of green tea features high-quality dried tea, well-prepared water, good tea ware and graceful actions. However, the key factor is to brew the tea with one's heart because only the truest heart can make the best pot of green tea. It may appear simple to brew a cup of green tea, but actually, it is quite difficult to simultaneously deal with the temperature of hot water, amount of dried tea, brewing duration, choice of tea ware, brewing times and water-refilling—crucial factors for brewing quality tea.

1. Temperature of Water

For brewing green tea, the temperature of water is the variable. It depends on the tea varieties classified by appearances, processing techniques, production seasons, production areas and tea plants. For example, the temperature of water is 60–65°C for tea powder, 70–75°C for Bi Luo Chun Tea, around 80°C for most high quality and famous brands and some can even be 85–90°C. The general principle is that it should be around 80°C for most high quality and famous varieties. For staple ones, it can be a little higher, (85–90°C). But there are also exceptions. For example, for high quality Liu An Gua Pian Tea processed from single leaves, the temperature should be around 85°C to give a mellow and fragrant brew. If the temperature is too high the high-quality and famous-variety leaves will be scorched and the liquid will be a little yellowish-green, appearing deteriorated or aged. If the temperature is too low, there will be very little fragrance and the taste will be light. Furthermore, the dried leaves will float on the surface for a longer time. A strainer will be necessary to separate the dregs.

2. Amount of Dried Tea

The amount of dried tea determines the strength of the tea liquid. If it is too much, the liquid will be too strong with a bitter and astringent taste; if it is too little, the liquid will be light and tasteless, without the true flavor. The amount of dried tea should be adjusted according to the volume and size of the teapots.

Principles governing the amount of dried tea:

1) Single teapot—the ratio of tea to water is 1:50.
2) Kettle for multiple cups and teapots—2–3g for each person.
3) The amount can be adjusted as per preference.

3. Brewing Duration

Steeping in hot water will make the dried tea leaves blossom. For a single pot, brew the tea for around 1 minute. For a tea kettle and cups or pots, the first brew should be around 30 seconds, and subsequently for 5–10 seconds more than the previous time. Another way to brew tea is with an inner-pot-equipped teapot (3-piece sets). The brewed leaves can be taken out to prevent overlong brewing.

4. Brewing Tea Ware

Transparent glass teapots, such as glass cups and glass kettles are convenient to watch the "dance of tea leaves" in the liquid. Other porcelain teapots, such as the covered bowl, porcelain cup and porcelain kettle, can also be used. Do not immediately cover pots or kettles to avoid scorching the tea.

Glass teacup

Glass tea kettle

Tiny teacup

Porcelain tea bowl

5. Methods of Putting Dried Tea

There are many ways of adding the dried tea.

The "top brewing" method: Warm the teapot, fill the teapot with hot water to around 70%, add the dried tea.
The "middle brewing" method: Warm the teapot, add the dried tea leaves into the teapot, add small amount of hot water to moisturize the tea leaves, add hot water to 70% full.
The "bottom brewing" method: Warm the teapot, add the dried tea into teapot, thereafter, fill the teapot up to 70% with the hot water.

The "top" (Bi Luo Chun Tea and Meng Ding Gan Lu Tea) and "middle" (Xi Hu Long Jing Tea, Huang Shan Mao Feng Tea and An Ji Bei Cha Tea) way are usually adopted in brewing high-quality green teas, while the "bottom" way is adopted to brew staple green teas. However, some high-quality green tea varieties, such as Tai Ping Hou Kui Tea and Liu An Gua Pian Tea adopt the "bottom" way.

6. Number of Brewings

Green tea leaves, especially high-quality ones, do not endure long brewing. High-quality green tea can be brewed for 2–3 times while the staple one for 3–4 times. When brewing in a single teapot, hot water should be refilled when the pot is about one-third or half full. Refilling when very little brewed liquid is left affects the strength of the next round. If the tea is being brewed in a covered bowl or teapot and poured into cups for drinking, add hot water only after the teapot is empty. Cups should be refilled only after the cups become empty.

Brewing Green Tea

1. Brewing Tai Ping Hou Kui in a Glass

Pre-brewing Preparations

Tea ware: Electric instant tea kettle, glass teapot, tea holder, tea towel, tea spoon, water container, etc.
Water: Fill the right amount of water in the electric instant tea kettle. Bring to boil. Cool down to 85°C, ready for use.

Note:
1 Take out Tai Ping Hou Kui Tea leaves with great care, or the fragile leaves will crumble.

2 It is better to use bigger porcelain teapots (kettles), above 10cm.

3 Tai Ping Hou Kui Tea is generally brewed in the "bottom brewing" way.

Brewing

1. Prepare the tea ware: Keep the tea ware ready for brewing.

2. Warm the teapot: Warm the glass by pouring a little water.

3. Drain the teapot: Drain the water into the water container, wipe water stains.

4. Adding tea leaves: Carefully spoon dried leaves into the glass.

5. Pour water: Fill the glass to 70% full with hot water.

6. Soak the leaves: Steep the tea for 1 minute.

2. Brewing Bi Luo Chun Tea in a Glass

Pre-brewing Preparations

Tea ware: Electric instant tea kettle, glass, tea holder, tea towel, tea spoons, water container, etc.
Water: Fill the right amount of water in an electric instant tea kettle. Bring to boil. Cool down to 85°C, ready for use.
Tea leaves: Add Bi Luo Chun Tea into the tea holder.

Note:

1. It is better to steep the fine and tender Bi Luo Chun Tea in water with temperature around 70–75°C.
2. Due to the overgrowth of fuzz around the petiole, it is normal to see seemingly turbid liquid while brewing Bi Luo Chun Tea.
3. Watch the "dance of leaves" while brewing.
4. This tea is generally brewed in the "top brewing" way.

Brewing

1. Prepare the tea ware: Keep the tea ware ready for brewing.

2. Warm the teapot: Warm the glass by pouring a little water.

3. Drain the teapot: Drain the water into the water container. Wipe the water stains.

4. Pour water: Fill the glass to 70% full.

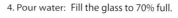

5. Adding tea leaves: Carefully spoon dried leaves of Bi Luo Chun Tea into the glass.

6. Soak the leaves: Steep the tea for 1 minute.

3. Brewing Zhu Ye Qing Tea in Borosilicate Glass Teapots

Pre-brewing Preparations

Tea ware: Electric instant tea kettle, borosilicate glass teapot, fairness cup, tea holder, tea spoon, water container, etc.

Water: Fill water in the electric instant tea kettle. Bring to boil.

Note:

1. The temperature of hot water should be around 80°C for brewing the flat and single-leaf Zhu Ye Qing Tea.

2. A large fairness cup can serve a "water-cooler."

3. The green tea will float on the surface of water around 1 minute before sinking to the bottom after absorption.

4. The single-leaf variety of green teas, such as Zhu Ye Qing Tea, Mei Tan Cui Ya Tea, Zi Yang Yin Zhen Tea and Kai Hua Long Ding Tea, etc. is generally brewed in the "middle brewing" way.

Tips

The "water-cooler" fairness cup will cool down the water to around 80°C.

Brewing

1. Prepare the tea ware: Keep the tea ware ready for brewing.

2. Warm the teapot: Pour hot water in the tea bowl.

3. Drain the water: Warm bowl covers with hot water for warming tea bowl, and then drain into the water container.

4 . Cool the water: Fill the fairness cup with hot water. Cool the temperature to 80°C.

5. Adding tea leaves: Carefully spoon dried leaves of Zhu Ye Qing Tea into the tea bowl.

6. Moisturize the tea-leaves: Pour a little hot water to moisturize the tea.

7. Pour water: Pour hot water from a height to fill bowls to 70%.

8. Soak the leaves: Steep the tea for 1 minute.

4. Brewing An Ji Bai Cha in Glass Tumblers

Pre-brewing Preparations

Tea ware: Electric instant tea kettle, glass tumbler, small sharable glass and cups, tea holder, tea towel, tea spoon, strainer, water container, etc.

Water: Pour water in the electric instant tea kettle. Bring to boil. Cool the hot water to 80°C, ready for use.

Tea leaves: Add the right amount of An Ji Bai Cha into the tea holder.

Note:

1. The leaves absorb water and open. The brewed leaves can turn light or greenish-white.

2. Brewing in glass tumblers one can appreciate the "greenish white" brewed leaves.

3. Green tea can be brewed for 3–4 times in a small pot and drunk in cups.

4. An Ji Bai Cha is generally brewed in the "middle brewing" way in a single cup, but the "bottom brewing" way is used to brew in pots.

Brewing

1. Prepare the tea ware: Keep the tea ware ready to brew.

2. Warm tea ware: Fill a little hot water into the glass teapot.

3. Warm fair mugs: Pour the boiled water from the kettle into the fairness cup.

4. Warm cups: Thereafter pour the hot water from fairness cup into each little cup.

5. Adding tea leaves: Carefully spoon An Ji Bai Cha into the glass teapots.

6. Soak the leaves: From a height, pour hot water into the teapots, and brew for 1 minute.

7. Drain water: Drain the water into the water container. Wipe water stains.

8. Strain tea liquid: Pour the brewed liquid into the fairness cup through the strainer.

9. Dividing liquid: Divide the liquid into each little glass cup to 70% full.

10. Appreciation: The tea is ready to drink.

5. Brewing Osmanthus Green Tea in a 3-piece Glass Teapot

Pre-brewing Preparations

Tea ware: Electric instant kettles, 3-piece glass teapot, tea holder, tea towel, tea spoon, etc.

Water: Boil the right amount of water. Cool the hot water to 85°C, ready for use.

Tea leaves: Add the right amount of Yun Wu Green Tea (or other brands) into the tea holder. Meanwhile keep aside dried osmanthus flowers.

Note:

1. While brewing green tea, a "scented tea" can be made by adding some dried flowers.
2. Staple green tea liquid will be strong, even bitter and astringent if brewed too long. To avoid this, use inner-pot-equipped teapot
3. The 3-piece glass teapot is portable and convenient.
4. Staple green tea is generally brewed in the "bottom brewing" way.

Brewing

1. Prepare tea ware: Keep the tea ware ready for brewing.

2. Prepare dried flowers: Add the right amount of dried osmanthus flowers and evenly mix with tea.

3. Warm teapot: Pour a little water in the glass teapot . Drain the water.

4. Adding tea leaves: Carefully spoon dried leaves of flower-and-tea-mix into the inner pot of glass teapot.

5. Soak the leaves: From a height, pour hot water into the teapot to 70% full, and brew for 1 minute.

6. Appreciation: The tea can be appreciated and drunk after uncovering glass teapot, placing the cover upside down on the tea desk, drawing out the inner-pots and putting it on the cover.

6. Brewing Long Jing Tea in Covered Bowls
Pre-brewing Preparations

Tea ware: Electric instant kettles, covered bowls, tea holder, tea-towels, tea spoon, water container, etc.

Water: Boil the right amount of water in an electric instant kettle. Cool the hot water to 80°C, ready for use.

Tea Leaves: Add Long Jing tea into the tea holder.

Note:

1. The bowls should be kept a little slanted and the covers a little open while brewing high-quality green tea so as not to over brew the tea leaves.
2. To brew scented Long Jing tea, mix a few dried chrysanthemum flowers.
3. Long Jing tea is generally brewed using the "middle brewing" method.

Tips

Making chrysanthemum Long Jing tea

Mix Long Jing tea and a few dried chrysanthemum flowers in a covered bowl.

Steep in 80°C hot water.Drink after the leaves blossom after absorption of water.

Brewing

1. Prepare tea ware: Keep the tea ware ready for brewing.

2. Warm tea ware: Pour a little hot water into covered bowl.

3. Drain water: Drain the used water into the water container and warm the cover with it.

4. Add tea leaves: Carefully spoon dried Long Jing tea leaves into the covered bowl.

5. Moisturize tea leaves: Pour a little hot water into the covered bowl to moisturize the tea leaves.

6. Pour water: Pour hot water into the covered bowl to 70% full.

7. Soak the leaves: Brew the tea keeping the cover slightly open for around 1 minute.

8. Appreciation: Savor the tea after the leaves absorb water.

7. Brewing Wu Yuan Ming Mei Tea in Tiny Porcelain Teapots

Pre-brewing Preparations

Tea ware: Electric instant kettles, tiny porcelain teapots, tea holder, tea towel, tea spoon, water containers, etc.

Water: Boil water in the electric instant kettle. Cool the water down to 80°C, ready for use.

Tea leaves: Add Wu Yuan Ming Mei Tea into the tea holder.

Note:
1. Brewing green tea in a blue porcelain teapot is a visual treat.
2. Wu Yuan Ming Mei Tea is generally brewed in the "middle" way.

Brewing

1. Prepare tea ware: Keep the tea ware ready for brewing.

2. Warm teapot: Pour a little hot water into the tiny porcelain teapot.

3. Drain water: Drain the water into the water container.

4. Add tea leaves: Carefully spoon dried Wu Yuan Ming Mei Tea leaves into the teapot.

5. Pour water: Fill the teapot to 70% full.

6. Appreciation: Brew for 1 minute. Your tea is ready.

8. Brewing Broadleaf Zao Chun Yin Ya Tea in Covered Bowls

Pre-brewing Preparations

Tea ware: Electric instant kettles, covered bowl, fairness cup, teapot, tea holder, tea spoon, tea folder, gourd-shaped strainer, wastewater container, etc.

Water: Boil water in the electric instant kettle. Cool the water down to 85°C, ready for use.

Tea leaves: Spoon broadleaf Zao Chun Yin Ya Tea into the tea holder.

Note:

1. Yunnan broadleaf green tea is characterized by fat and sturdy buds and leaves with white fuzz, rich in elements, enduring brew. It is best to brew in a kettle (or covered bowl) and drunk from cups.

2. Yunnan broadleaf Zao Chun Yin Ya Tea used here is a variety of sun-dried green tea.

3. Moisturize the sun-dried green tea before formal brewing. The second and third brewing are the best brews.

4. The brewing duration should not be too long in the first brewing, but should be steeped more in later brews.

5. Sun-dried Yunnan broadleaf green tea is generally brewed using the "bottom brewing" method.

6. The temperature of water for brewing low quality broadleaf green tea should be higher than the high-quality ones.

Brewing

1. Tea ware: Keep the tea ware ready for brewing.

2. Warm teapot: Pour a little hot water into the covered bowl.

3. Warm fair mug: Pour the water used to warming the bowl into the fairness cup.

4. Warm tea cup: Pour the water in the fairness cup into every tea cup.

5. Drain water: Hold the teacups with tea tong and drain the water.

6. Add leaves: Carefully spoon dried broadleaf Zao Chun Yin Ya Tea leaves into the covered bowl.

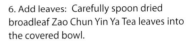

7. Moisturize tea leaves: Pour hot water into bowl to moisturize the tea.

8. Add water: From a height, fill the bowl with hot water.

9. Formal brewing: Cover the bowl for 15–20 seconds.

10. Pour tea liquid: Pour the brewed liquid into the fairness cup.

11. Distribute the liquid: Distribute the liquid into each tea cup to 70% full.

12. Appreciation: The tea is ready for drinking after brewing for 1 minute.

9. Brewing Green Tea Powder in Porcelain Tea Bowl

Pre-brewing Preparations

Tea ware: Electric instant tea kettle, big porcelain tea bowl, tea brush, tea spoon, etc.

Water: Boil water in the electric instant tea kettle. Cool the hot water down to 65°C, ready for use.

Tea powder: Prepare the right amount of tea powder.

Note:

1. Brew tea powder in temperately hot water.
2. Seal the package immediately after drawing out the tea powder to prevent absorption of moisture.
3. A spoonful of tea powder is enough for one teapot.
4. Add the tea powder to the yogurt to get "green tea yogurt."

Making "green tea yogurt"

Add the appropriate amount of tea powder into the yogurt.

Mix evenly and pour into the porcelain bowl.

Brewing

1. Tea ware: Keep the tea ware ready for brewing.

2. Warm teapot: Pour a little hot water into the porcelain tea bowl.

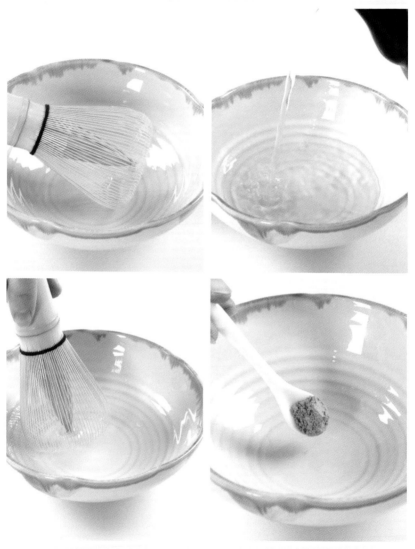

3. Drain water: Warm the porcelain tea bowl and tea mixer. Drain the water.

4. Add tea powder: Spoon the appropriate amount into the porcelain tea bowl.

5. Pour water: Add a little hot water into porcelain tea bowl.

6. Make paste: Use the tea mixer to mix the tea powder and hot water to make a paste.

7. Steeping: Pour hot water into the porcelain tea bowl and continue to mix.

8. Appreciation: The tea is ready to be drunk after mixing evenly.

Column 8 Tea Polyphenols Free Radicla

After drinking tea, the tea polyphenols inside the body will work on the excess free radicals in the body. As a result, the tea polyphenols and the excess free radicals will be disposed out of the body. Helping the body to get rid of the excess radicals contributes to improving the health and deferring aging.

What are free radicals?

Free radicals are by-products of metabolism in the human body. With aging, changing of environments, cigarette smoking, pollution, radiations from computers or TV, depression, the human body produces excess free radicals that are more than the body can handle. The excess free radicals deteriorate or damage cell functions of biomacromolecules in some substances such as proteins, and unsaturated fatty acids, consequently, they will accelerate aging and cause sickness.

How do tea polyphenols clean free radicals?

As the essence of tea, tea polyphenols is the general name for phenolic substances and their derivatives in fresh tea leaves, and it is the most soluble element in fresh leaves (usual content is above 15%, the highest is 40%). The first step of processing green tea—deactivation—deactivates the enzymes in the fresh leaves, to prevent the oxidation of polyphenolic enzymes. Therefore the tea plyphenols content in green tea is higher than that of other tea varieties.

Sensory Evaluation of Tea

Part 5

This part tells about the evaluation of green tea from a professional perspective. For the daily tea drinker, there is no need to strictly follow the evaluation procedure prescribed. But it always helps to learn how to evaluate green tea in the professional way.

Sensory evaluation is a way of inspecting tea quality conducted through sensory appraisals. Professional tea evaluators evaluate the quality through the four senses (sight, taste, smell and touch). In history, Lu Yu's the *Classic of Tea* records the shape, color, size and usage of tea evaluation instruments, as well as the specifications of roasting, cooking, hot water and drinking. It describes the standards and specifications of color, fragrance and taste. *The Record of Tea* (Cai Xiang, Song Dynasty, 1012–1067) is a book mostly on tea evaluation. It records the best tea features "the brilliant fuzzy petiole," "the truest fragrance" and "the most sweet and mellow taste"— evaluation standards at that time. In addition, in the Song Dynasty, people performed "Tea Contests" (a contest of tea evaluation) and "Tea Division" (a display of the art of brewing tea). Such activities, too, were kinds of tea evaluation.

Although most tea drinkers are amateur tea evaluators, evaluation is necessary while buying tea. Standards and methods of evaluation are demanding when you have to select the best among various brands.

Sensory evaluation of tea is classified into normal, pattern-matching, contrasting and secret code evaluations, of which the former two are the most used ones.

Experienced tea growers or traders evaluate tea quality by their experience. Usually, they take a handful of tea out in the light. They closely look at the color and appearance, thereafter hold it close to mouth and exhale into the tea leaves. Then, quickly they hold the hand to the nose to inhale the fragrance. Alternately, they take a handful of tea leaves on a tea sample plate. They hold the plate in one hand while touching the tea leaves with the other. Every year, during the tea-marketing season, tea traders take a handful of sample tea to brew and evaluate before purchase.

I. Evaluating Green Tea

Pre-brewing Preparations

Tea ware for evaluation: Electric instant tea kettle, plate, pot, bowl, soup spoon, soup cup, electronic scale, blank paper sheets, timers, used-liquid holders.

Water: Boil the appropriate amount of water in the electric instant tea kettle, ready for use.

Warm: Warm pots, plates, soup spoon and soup cup. Place in proper order, ready for use.

Take 200g of green tea onto plate.

Place a small piece paper on electronic scale (set on zero).

Note:
1. Boiling water should be used for brewing green tea; brewing duration is 5 minutes.
2. While straining the liquid, keep the lip of tea pot upside down, and place on the edge of the bowl; pour the entire the liquid out.
3. The mouthful of liquid used for sensing the taste is usually not swallowed, but spit out into the used-liquid holder.
4. Breathe in the fragrance three times for hot, warm and cool smell, respectively, for only 3 seconds each time. Excessively long smelling will desensitize the nose.
5. If necessary, write an evaluation report after finishing the evaluation.

Brewing

1.Sampling: Take the sample tea with the thumb, index finger and middle finger.

2. Weighing: Weigh 3g sample tea on the electronic scale.

3. Add tea leaves: Remove teapot cover and put the 3g sample tea into pot.

4. Pour water: Pour hot water into pot to the brim and cover. Brew for 5 minutes.

5. Warming soup spoon: Pour a half cupful of hot water into the soup pot to warm the soup spoon.

6 Straining: After brewing for 5 minutes, strain the liquid out into bowl.

7 Evaluating liquid color: Evaluate the liquid color, and note the tea dregs.

8 Evaluating liquid color: Stir the soup spoon once in the direction shown, and take it out.

9 Evaluating liquid color: Wait for the tea dregs to completely settle at the bottom so that the luminance, depth, clarity, etc., can be seen.

10 Inhaling fragrance: Hold the liquid-filled pot in one hand, and with the other, remove the cover slightly. Bring nose close to pot and inhale the fragrance to evaluate the degree of purity, strength and duration, etc.

11. Tasting: Take a spoonful of liquid with the soup spoon.

12 Tasting: Take the liquid without swallowing. Swirl in the mouth to let the taste buds in the tongue evaluate the strength, purity and freshness. Spit the liquid out.

13. Evaluating tea immersion: Pour the brewed leaves onto the reverse side of the pot cover or in another clean bowl. Add some water, and evaluate the degree of tenderness, contours and color, etc. of the leaves.

II. Evaluation Instruments

Where tea evaluation is a scientifically important activity, more attention is paid to the specifications and pragmatic functions of the instruments, while for daily brewing tea, aesthetic appeal is more important.

To evaluate tea in your home, specialized pots and scales are the essential instruments, while the others can be replaced by household utensils.

For a professional evaluation chamber, the essential instruments include:

○ **Evaluation Pot**
It is a specially made cylindrical porcelain pot used for brewing tea and smelling the fragrance. It has a saw-tooth lip at the mouth of the pot (a hole in the cover of traditional pot), through which the liquid is filtered out when the pot is overturned. The volume is 150ml. For evaluating Oolong tea use a bell-shaped pot; the volume is exactly 110ml.

Coverd cup used as evaluation pot

The saw-tooth lip at the mouth opposite to the handle

○ **Bowl**

It is a specially made white porcelain bowl used for holding brewed liquid and evaluating liquid color. The mouth is wider, and the volume is 250ml. Bell-shaped bowl should match with bell-shaped pot to evaluate Oolong tea; the volume a little less than that for other teas. The serial numbers at the bottom of pots and bowls should match.

Bowl

○ **Soup pot and soup spoon**

The soup pot is a small white porcelain bowl used for setting the soup spoon and strainer, etc. It should be warmed before use. The soup spoon is a white porcelain spoon used for spooning the stewed liquid. The volume is 5ml and also should be warmed before use. Use the soup spoon to sip the liquid to sense the taste.

Soup pot and soup spoon

○ Plate

Square or rectangular, the plate is made of odor-free wood, painted white, or sometimes bamboo or plastic. It is used for evaluating appearance of the dried tea leaves. One corner has an opening for pouring tea leaves out.

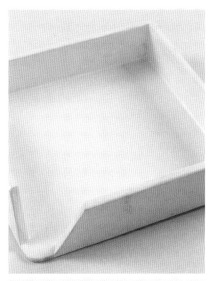

Plate

○ Scale

The scale is usually a table balance or an electronic scale with an accuracy of 0.1g. It should be set on zero and properly balanced before weighing the tea.

Scale

○ Timer

It is usually an auto-alarm timer or a 5-minute timer. It can also be replaced by a cell phone or watch, etc.

Timer

○ Brewed tea leaves container

Traditionally, the container is a black-painted square wooden plate. Today, it usually is a stainless steel or white porcelain plate; sometimes pot cover is used. In tea evaluations at home, we can evaluate the brewed leaves in a white porcelain plate or in a bowl holding clean water.

Brewed leaves container

○ Kettle (Electric instant tea kettle)

Usually it is a large stainless steel or aluminum kettle used for boiling water.

For professional evaluation, the necessary instruments include:

○ Evaluation platforms

Evaluation platforms are of two kinds: dry platform and humid platform. The former is used for setting sample tea container, plate, scale, etc., and serves for evaluating the appearance of dried tea. The surface should be smooth and black. The latter is used for setting pot, bowl, soup spoon, soup pot, timer, etc., and serves for evaluating the liquid color, taste, fragrance and brewed leaves. The surface should be impermeable and white, have an open corner for the liquid to flow.

○ Cupboard for samplings

The cupboard is used for keeping sample containers and is usually white.

○ Straining spoon

This is a stainless steel or nylon spoon, used to filter the tea dregs in the liquid.

○ Evaluated liquid container

This container is used to keep tea dregs and liquid. Use it to spit the liquid during evaluation.

○ Kitchen cabinet

This cabinet is used for keeping pot, bowl and soup pot, etc.

○ Evaluation form

Instruments used in household tea evaluation can be replaced by household utensils. For example, timer by a cell phone or watch, etc., liquid container for spitting by water container and soup pot and spoon by clean and odor-free white porcelain table wares, etc.

Requirements for the evaluators

A professional evaluator should be highly sensitive to smell, sight, taste, touch, etc. He should be free of body odor and chronic diseases, such as hepatitis, pneumonia, etc.

The evaluator is the most important "instrument" in sensory evaluation. The evaluator needs to develop a good habit of living, which specifically means no smoking, no alcohol, should not eat strong-flavored foods, such as green onion and garlic, or oversweet or fried foods, and monitor intake of medicines, such as antibiotics and proprietary Chinese medicine. If one has taken unsuitable foods or medicines, they cannot take part in tea evaluation for the next 4 hours.

In addition, the evaluator should wash hands before evaluation work. He must be free from foreign odors of cosmetics, such as handcare cream, perfume, etc. All in all, the evaluator should in the optimal condition to evaluate.

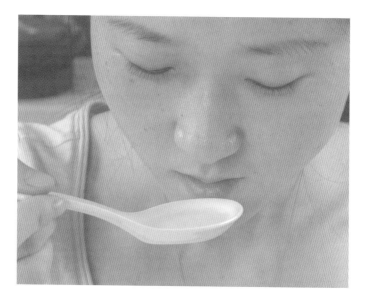

III. Tea Evaluation Procedure and Scoring

1. Specific Procedure

○ **Sampling**

Take a 200–250g typical sample of tea and put it onto the evaluation plate.

Sampling means to take a small amount of the tea from a bulk of tea for evaluation. The method of picking the sample directly affects the results of evaluation.

○ **Assessing appearance**

In this process, the shape, color, contour, size, thickness, fineness, tenderness, etc., of the dried tea will be assessed.

Before assessing the appearance, the evaluator should take a "sample sieving plate." This means to move the evaluation plate back and forth, with one hand holding the outlet end and the other the opposite end so that the dried tea leaves can be concentrated in three layers.

At the end of this assessment, write down the appraisals.

○ **Weighing sample**

Weigh 3g sample tea on the scale. Put it into the evaluation cup.

After the tea has been concentrated in three layers, pick up a little more than 3g dried leaves with the thumb, index finger and middle finger. Pick the tea in such a way that all the three layers are represented. In addition, the weight should be a little more than 3g (less should not be used as sample).

Be careful while picking leaves, because the dried leaves can break into pieces giving inaccurate results.

○ **Steeping**

Fill boiling water into the appreciation cup to the brim. Ensure there is no overflowing. Cover the cup and brew for 5 minutes.

Bring the water to boil before brewing. It should be purified or demineralized, for too many minerals in the water will affect the results of evaluation. Do not overboil the water or use tap water. Before brewing, wash and dry the appreciation cups, bowls and spoons used in this process and put them on the humid platform according to their serial numbers. Uncover the appreciation cup. If many cups of tea are evaluated at the same time, only the first cup should be timed. After pouring water into the last cup, pour a half cup of hot water into the soup cup.

Brewing

○ **Straining liquid**

Filter the brewed liquid in the appreciation cup into the appreciation bowl. After 5 minutes, in sequence, pick up the cups from the first to the last, put them upside down on the bowls so as to filter the liquid out. Take care not to let the liquid overflow the bowls. The actions should be accurate, or the evaluation results of liquid, taste, and fragrance will be affected.

Filtering liquid

○ Assessing liquid color

Assess the degree of thickness, brightness, clarity, etc. by sight.

The liquid color can be assessed when the liquid has been filtered out and the appreciation cup has been taken out from the appreciation bowl. Before assessing, the tea dregs in the liquid should be separated from the liquid with a strainer and taken out; or swirl the soup spoon once in one direction to concentrate the dregs at the bottom.

Assessing liquid color

○ Smelling fragrance

Assess the types, concentration and purity by smelling.

To inhale the fragrance, the evaluator should hold the appreciation cup full of the liquid in one hand, and keeping the cover half open with the other hand, inhale the fragrance three times respectively at hot, warm and cool moments; the duration is 3 seconds for each smell. The results will be affected if the time is more than 3 seconds.

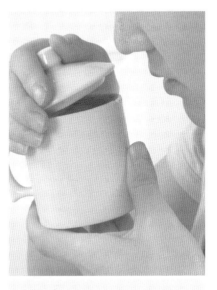

Smelling fragrance

○ **Tasting**

Sense the degree of concentration, level of pleasant taste, freshness and purity, etc. of the liquid.

Take about a spoonful of liquid with the white porcelain soup spoon from the appreciation bowl into the mouth. Swirl it round the tongue to completely and properly sense the taste. To taste, first hold the liquid in the mouth; breathe in noisily. Do not swallow the liquid but spit out into the used-liquid container. Wash the spoon in the soup cup, and in sequence, taste the other cup of tea. Tasting should be carried out immediately after assessing the fragrance; the appropriate temperature of the liquid is 50°C.

○ **Assessing brewed leaves**

Assess the degree of tenderness, smoothness, broken or unbroken, and purity, etc. of tea leaves by sight and touch.

Put all the leftover leaves on the reverse surface of the brewed leaves container, or on the white porcelain plate filled with clean water. Thereafter assess the color, contour, purity, tenderness, and finally, touch them with fingers to feel the softness, thickness, etc.

○ **Writing evaluation appraisals**

After the evaluation, fill the evaluation form with the results in the professional terms. Compute and score according to weight numbers of various tea categories.

The aspects of sensory tea evaluation include appearance, liquid color, fragrance, taste and infusion. The evaluation of dried tea is also known as dry evaluation, and that of liquid color, fragrance, taste, brewed leaves collectively called humid evaluation. The quality of dried leaves depends on comprehensive evaluation results; similar tea brands or varieties should be brewed and evaluated in pairs. In conclusion, sensory tea evaluation should be strictly conducted in accordance with the professional procedure to get accurate results.

2. Scoring in Professional Evaluation

In daily life, the most-consumed are the high-quality and staple green tea varieties. The former are evaluated by assessing the "five aspects"—appearance, liquid color, fragrance, taste and infusion. The evaluation is done in the process mentioned before.

In some evaluation activities in China, evaluators adopt the percentile scoring and weighted scoring models. In the former model, when the score totals 100, the actual result will have been computed by adding the score of each item in evaluating graded sample tea or standard sample tea. In the latter model, the weight is determined by the degree of each aspect. The weightage of high-quality tea is: appearance 30%, liquid color 10%, fragrance 25%, taste 25%, tea immersion 10%.

Sample Form of Scoring for Evaluation of High-Quality Tea						
	Appearance	Liquid Color	Fragrance	Taste	Brewed Leaves	Total
Ratio(%)	30	10	25	25	10	100
Scoring	90	90	92	90	88	—
Results	27	9	23	22.5	8.8	90.3

Evaluation appraisals can be written down in accordance with the results. Sometimes a mere score cannot completely illustrate the quality, therefore appraisals should also be considered in evaluation of tea quality. The professional evaluation terms are essential and they should be used in appraisals as accurately as possible.

Professional tea evaluation method can be adopted in daily tea evaluation to have a better understanding of the quality. Although a household tea evaluation does not use every instrument and item, the major processes should follow the professional specifications.

IV. Issues Critical to Green Tea Evaluation

Professional evaluators are more familiar with evaluation procedures than the evaluations conducted in households. Some aspects, such as temperature of the hot water or the brewing duration would not be accurately controlled, and the evaluation results would be affected.

Tea evaluation and techniques of tea making are two different processes. The former means to evaluate quality by technical standards; while the later is to display the art of tea making. The following points need to be kept in mind to better understand tea evaluation:

○ Boiling water should be used to brew the sample tea.

Keep the water prepared for brewing the sample tea boiling for a while before pouring into the teapot. Especially in winter, just-boiled water will affect evaluation results. Meanwhile, if various tea varieties are evaluated at the same time, a big kettle should be used to boil water to ensure enough water.

○ The water used in evaluation should be purified or demineralized.

Stir up the tea leaves with the water force to allow the leaves to float and sink repetitively in the liquid so as to have more tea soup from the brewing; when the liquid amounts to the pot level of 70–78% full, lower the position of the pot and pour out the liquid slowly into the cups without spilling.

○ The tea leaves sample should be picked at one pinch.

○ The weight of the sample can be more but never less; the sample should contain the upper, middle and bottom layers of the tea leaves.

○ Assessing liquid color before assessing fragrance, taste and brewed leaves.

○ In humid evaluation, liquid color assessing should be performed before that of fragrance, taste and brewed leaves, for liquid color depends on the water temperature, light, size of evaluation bowls, deposits at the bottom.

When tasting liquid of various teas, wash the soup spoon in the soup pot, and rinse the mouth with fresh water before taking another liquid so that the taste is not carried to the next liquid. Taste can be assessed many times to achieve the right result.

○ Duration for inhaling fragrance is around 3 seconds.

The duration of each inhalation should not be longer than 5 seconds, or the evaluator will become insensitive to the fragrance.

○ The liquid remaining in the evaluation cup should be filtered out.

○ The ratio of tea to water is 1:50

○ The ratio of tea to water is 1:50, brew 3g tea in a 150ml cup, but never 4g tea with 200ml, etc.

○ Wash the evaluation instruments.

At the end of the evaluation, wash the instruments. Pay special attention to the saw-shaped outlet of the evaluation cup. Keep the washed instruments upside down hooked on a shelf in the closet to dry. Collect and store sample tea properly to prevent deterioration through moisturization.

References

Shen Peihe, et al. *A Guide to Tea Evaluation*. Beijing: China Agricultural University Press, 1998.

Lu Songhou, Shi Zhaopeng. *Evaluation and Inspection of Tea Varieties*. Beijing: China Agriculture Press, 2001.

Wang Guangzhi. *Tea Varieties and Famous Local Brands in China*. Beijing: China Agriculture Press, 2003.

Cheng Qikun. *Chinese Green Tea*. Guangzhou: Guangdong Tourism Publishing House, 2005.

Zhu Yongxing, Wang Yuefei. *Study on Tea Medicine*. Hangzhou: Zhejiang University Press, 2005.

Liu Xin. *Questions and Answers on Organic Tea Production and Management*. Beijing: Golden Shield Press, 2003.

Acknowledgments

Beijing Gengxiang Tea Co., Ltd

Xiaoyang's Xi Hu Long Jing Tea Line

Xishan Bi Luo Chun Tea Factory (Fang Meng Tea Line) of Wu County, Jiangsu Province

Huangshan Yipingming Tea Line

Beijing Diqishijianshi Tea Center

Zhenfeng Tea Line

Zhenfengqiao Tea Co., Ltd

Wang Guangzhi Tea Line

Anhui Jingzhai Qifu Organic Tea Factory (Beijing Office)

Beijing Yunqing Tea Line

Zhou Mei's Xin Yang Mao Jian Tea

Shaanxi Dongyu Tea Industry Co., Ltd

Instrument Provider: Li Hong
                            Li Mei